Key Thoughts for Talks

by
Reed L. Hart

Published by
HAWKES PUBLISHING, INC.

3775 South 500 West
Salt Lake City, Utah 84115
Tel. (801) 262-5555

ISBN 0-89036-105-3

Typesetting
by
HAWKES PUBLISHING, INC.

TABLE OF CONTENTS

GOOD MORNING! This is a beautiful day and it belongs to you; it's special and yours to claim for it has never been lived before. With its passing, there comes one less day to live, but one more to recall.

GRAVITY

Gravity is a force that tends to draw all bodies in the earth's sphere towards the center of the earth. Its pull is constant and relates to the material things of the universe. Gravity, however, is powerless and has no influence over the spiritual part of man, over his thoughts, his conscience, his expressions, desires and choices.

The rate of acceleration of gravity on a falling object is about thirty-two feet a second. Many have learned to live with it, while others have died trying to understand it. Man can't get along without it. It keeps him earth bound. Gravity claims all earthly bodies for its own. It has the last word with the material aspects of the human family, but it lacks the power to contain the soul. It may keep things together on earth, but it's deficient in power to keep the spirit of man from soaring heavenward.

When the earthly life of man is used up, his body gravitates into and becomes a part of the elements of the earth. It returns to the home from whence it came, while the spirit gravitates or returns to its place of residence to fulfill and continue its progress. On the drawing boards of life there comes a point in time when the force of gravity must give up the properties of the body to the power of the spirit. The combination of the two makes up the immortal soul of man.

The first law of life is to live, the first law of death is to live again.

HIDDEN BEAUTY

One of the most expensive flowers in the floral shop today is the orchid. This flower is considered a symbol of luxury. Its beauty and light bluish-red colors become its credentials, yet the original birthplace of the orchid is the dense forest jungle. This beautiful flower was discovered and moved from its hidden birthplace to bloom in high places among men, bringing joy to the lovers of flowers around the world. The forest could no longer claim the orchid for its own, and now its loveliness belongs to the people.

There is hidden beauty everywhere, waiting to be discovered...to be seen and appreciated. There are some people who see something beautiful locked up in the lowly sagebrush, while others look, but fail to catch the elegance and beauty of the rose. As with the hidden orchid of the jungle, there is also beauty to be seen within the heart of every person.

A kind word, a good deed performed, or a pleasant smile, as with flowers and plant life, spring up in the most unlikely places for the blessings of people. Happiness and uplifting things are bound up in friends, and friends are the flowers of charm found growing by the "side of the road." To live without friends is to exist without sunshine. Some growing plants soon die without the sun. Flowers and friends bring a fullness to living...they speak. Each have a story to tell and within their identity are the seeds for tomorrow's bloom, designed for continuation of life. Springtime is planting time followed by a season for the gathering.

It has been said that a flower is "God's greatest creation without a soul." Flowers in their short season reach perfection, but God in his wisdom has provided man with an eternity to perfect the beauty of his soul.

HIDDEN TREASURES

Locked within the silence of the soul sleeps a spiritual force waiting and ready to emerge and speak out. It's a hidden treasure of talents and gifts anxious to reach out and penetrate, bringing joy into the lives of others. When the power of love touches the soul, there comes a change in the life style of man. He takes on new dimensions, he breathes and takes control, moving up to a higher level of performance. As one moves forward having been touched by the spirit of love and fellowship, his vision opens up to greater things and events so vital to salvation. Man becomes a part in creating new surroundings, new environments and in the process leaves behind the old. It is then that he becomes different, standing out from the crowd, blending into and sustaining the laws of the kingdom so basic to eternal happiness, where the promise of joy abounds.

A noted writer has said: "Give love a chance and it will perfect everything it touches. If you have no other quality than the quality of love, you can succeed with it alone. Without love, even though you may possess all knowledge, you fail."

The Gospel of Jesus Christ...restored, is the Gospel of love. Give it a chance and it will perfect everything it touches. It's a working process wherein he who lives the law may in the eternities become as God is. There is no greater incentive and challenge offered to the children of men than to become like Him.

Life is the workshop for development of the soul—during the process we outgrow many things, but we shall never outgrow the need for one another. The hour spent helping another is one less to live, but a treasured hour to remember.

THE HOME

Only when parents teach their children correct principles relating to God, Country, and friends living across the way will there come an in-depth love and richness of beauty to the home...in a setting where peace abounds with an unfolding oneness of resolve and understanding.

A cross section and the moral character within the home makes up the going power of nations...bringing a balance to their position of strength for a continuation. A nation's future relates more to its people and their way of life than in the abundance of factories, farms and industry.

When man begins to understand the nature and functions of the spirit as it relates to destiny, he then begins to understand the inner workings and finer parts of himself...his attitudes in building a happy home.

The gift of truth is the purpose of living and the reason for life. When values are recognized and understood, they fall into their proper place and life takes on new meaning. It is then that man learns what he will accept and what he will reject...what he lives for and what he must die for...that death is the result of living; that a fullness of death in the Lord is the purpose of his having come this way.

Only when "sin is ignored and dies untasted" will there come new dimensions into the life of man and joy to the home.

THE IDEAL TIME

The progressive minded people working on farms, in factories or business are constantly looking for the individual with a new idea. Good ideas generate new business, new opportunities, and opportunities become the life blood of progress calling for action in the "now."

An idea is a quality in time, an opportunity looking for a sponsor. When a new concept or idea comes to light and is taken hold of and developed into a new product, people remember only that someone "delivered the goods." Society isn't concerned with the problems and "labor pains" encountered along the way.

This life is short on guarantees and long on opportunities. When an opportunity comes, it never seems to appear on a day that is considered as the "ideal time." The "right time" to begin a project is no respector of circumstances...of a person's frame of mind, his finance or physical well-being. To recognize opportunity isn't always easy. It may show up in disguise, it's often seen only in work clothes, yet it's always on standby waiting to be challenged into action. New ideas are anxious to come under new management, to be seized by enthusiastic "advance men" with vision and determination.

When an "idea is born" and begins to breathe and grow, that's the ideal time to take hold and act.

After years of struggle Elias Howe invented an amazing machine. It would do 250 stitches per minute. It was called a "sewing machine." When it was demonstrated, the people responded by saying: "It has no practical use. This machine will throw thousands out of work." This was the year 1854. Everyone who saw the machine admired it, but no one bought it, and it nearly rusted away before the American women accepted it. At the death of his wife Howe was so poor it was necessary to borrow clothes to attend her funeral. Years later, however, things changed, and from the royalties of this invention, Elias Howe received four thousand dollars each day for several years. It was a well-earned reward for his patience and determination to carry on.

Had Mr. Howe waited for ideal conditions or delayed his invention until the American woman demanded a sewing machine, or for someone to financially underwrite him, or had he put off the urge to develop this idea that was to lighten the burden of women the world over, his name would have been lost in the file of unknown inventors.

In the year of 1456 after many years of struggle and financial difficulties, John Gutenberg introduced to the world for the first time a copy of a Latin Bible. The Bible was available to the public because of his invention and process of printing with "movable type."

Pious souls and religious leaders were shocked with the "devil's work." "The scriptures would now be available to the common people, and they in their ignorance would desecrate the Bible." It was an invasion into the profession of ministers who for centuries had reserved the right to read and interpret the word of God for their congregations.

The time was right to revolutionize the process of printing, but to Gutenberg the situation wasn't ideal. He had a series of lawsuits and disappointments causing a breakdown in health. Had he waited for this generation to demand a new process of printing to enlighten the common man in the field of learning, his contribution to the world would have been forever lost.

The greatest loss is the talent that is never awakened, the dignity and power of thought that is never used; a needed and fulfilling love that is never given.

IT'S YOUR MOVE

Today is for your use if you would like to make something of yourself. The Creator of heaven and earth has placed here an abundance of things for the needs of man...oxygen to breathe, water to drink, soil to till, riches of the earth to uncover. He has given man an inventory of goods with which to erect homes, build cities, and construct bridges for others who follow to safely pass over. He has provided mountains to climb and oceans to navigate. Man has been blessed with the vision to see and a mind to think, a voice to speak, and ears for communication. He has been given the potentials for the fullness of life with an understanding heart and a vibrant spirit that never dies.

Man is the spiritual offspring of God. If he were in a position to retrace his lineage, he would in time come face to face with his Father in heaven. If there is a "now," there is a before.

On this circular way of life there are many things to gain, and there are great risks involved. One who becomes careless with his life and loses his soul has lost it all. Those who keep their souls intact, in harmony with the useful and pleasant things provided along the way, are the winners. They will henceforth travel among the elect. They are at the point of arriving. Their names will be engraved on the tablets of eternity never to be erased, indicating they have proven themselves and risen above the weakness of the flesh. Their joy will come in knowing they have used up, with a fullness, the gifts and talents the Lord endowed them with.

To live out a life isn't easy. Often questions are asked: "What things in life should we hold on to? What must we let go of? By what standards do we measure? Should we run or pass the ball? By what authority are we judged?" We may safely hold on to that which enriches the soul and brings joy to the heart. Unless that which is reached for carries the ingredients that edify and widen the desire to move up and add new dimensions to living, and unless it has a permanence that contains itself, it may be dropped with safety. Values of permanence never fail, they have no bounds and never disintegrate.

In the process of living and getting along with others, man cannot escape the presence of himself, for it's the nearest thing to him. Joy comes within from beautifying the things which he touches as it relates to helping others. No deeds are so small and insignificant, that to the soul of man, it has no meaning.

Through the goodness of the Lord man is given much, yet he keeps so little. Many things that emerge to the surface and appear to be good are sometimes deceptive and block out that which is best. Integrity of purpose in building a life that is acceptable to the Lord is the highest ideal to be attained. It stands alone. To bring a fulfillment to that spiritual and living part of man is the purpose for which the plan of life and salvation was organized and set in motion.

KEEP MOVING

It has been said that a steam engine uses up about ninety percent of its potential starting power to get seventy-five cars rolling down the railroad track. Yet to keep the train moving it takes only five percent. The engine has in reserve about eighteen times the starting power over the going power. The secret of efficiency and performance is to keep the train moving. Without starting power an engine's going power becomes imprisoned and is confined to a condition of helplessness...it soon rusts away.

Desire and incentive is the inner drive that awakens man to new adventures. The thirst to satisfy this inner urge is the power that drives him forward. When incentive stops, the going power in man is cut and life begins to corrode.

But when man with enthusiasm keeps his cargo moving towards destination, he can expect the windfall of success. Only as he wastes his time and energies, leaving unused talents on the sidetrack of life, will his soul decay and rust away. Only in keeping the throttle of enthusiasm open, while clearing the tracks of obstacles ahead, will he come into his own, bringing the cargo home.

The prime time of life for making the right start and picking up momentum is in the moving present. Tomorrow's going power is untouchable, its usefulness isn't cast for the present. But today's greatest challenge is acquiring abilities equal to the unlimited opportunities as they present themselves in the "now."

THE HEART TRANSPLANT

Much has been written about the heart specialist and the success in removing deficient hearts and replanting new ones.

To receive a new heart isn't something untried. It was first introduced to the world in the words of the Lord when he said, "A new heart will I give thee."

To receive a spiritual restoration of the heart doesn't call for a battery of doctors and equipment. It calls for spiritual renewal; for a change in attitude, for dedication and reshaping of the soul into a oneness with the uplifting things of life.

When the Lord said, "I am the way, the truth and the life..." it made obsolete all other ways. His way is His gift to life. His house is an open house, His truth isn't reserved for a select few; it's the treasure of all men.

The most tragic death is to die spiritually.

The best exercise for the heart is bound up in the process of getting the right things going on earth. Our Father's business is big business. Under his management it's the only going concern where profits are guaranteed. He has the know-how of doing more with our life than we.

When the spirit is right with the Lord, we come under new management.

It's on the scale of values within the soul that the Great Physician measures blood pressures to calculate the needs of the heart. Transplanting new hearts through the skills of medicine merely adds anxiety to the gift of borrowed time for a short period, but a spiritual transformation of the soul, of he who has been walking in darkness of the truth over the years, extends life beyond the boundaries of time.

The most beautiful life is the spiritual life.

THE GAME OF CHECKERS

It is difficult to find someone on this circular planet who doesn't know how to play the game of checkers. The history of the game goes back forty centuries.

The game has many similarities to the game called "life." Both contests are most interesting, full of challenges and uncertainties. In life, as with checkers, the opponent across the board could be the player called "time." Each day becomes a move on the checkerboard of life, and every move affects the outcome and direction of every other move. The satisfaction of the game is evident when the right moves are made, when the best talents and traits are put into position of command; when every move is made as if it were the last. It's a suspense game. And all too often before the next anticipated play is made, "time"...the king of the game...calls the signal and the struggle ends. A story is told. Other players take up the challenge and the encounter goes on.

On the checkerboard, or the playing field, the riches of life are waiting to be claimed. They are bound up and related to work. Dr. Charles Mayo had a motto hung in his office. "There is no fun like work." Work is life. Life is a distance that must be traveled, a goal that must be reached. The experience of living is a continuous school master, whose lessons must be learned, out of which the rewards for having lived are conferred by the Divine Giver. Man is indebted.

The creativity of man is developed best in the workshop of life. If out of this laboratory of activity comes a high quality performance, there follows a fullness of joy. The richness of the earth is given man to take care of; to water the plants and cultivate the fields. He is its servant. If he produces an untarnished crop, the sustaining powers of the harvest are his to keep. He is enriched. He has been given a slice of life.

MAKING PROGRESS

A world famous cellist, at the age of eighty-three, was asked why he continued to practice several hours each day. He replied: "I think I'm making progress."

There is nothing quite so satisfying and delightful in combatting the pearls of retirement and old age, as meeting head-on with new challenges; fulfilling that inner urge and desire to reach out into new fields of self-discovery. Happiness comes in bringing to the surface unused talents, using them in new settings for reaching uplifting goals, cultivating and improving, letting mistakes feed upon themselves. The unwasted years are the years that give an account for growth and progress.

Happiness is a guaranteed product...only as long as one keeps on the move, doing things uplifting...becoming involved with something that grows and ascends towards the realm of spiritual awakenings. The Savior held the secret...he set the pattern...he "went about doing good."

Getting lost in doing good is the golden key for finding oneself. New discoveries unfold. Helping others sets the tone for living, it refines the spirit and enriches the soul.

Man knows what is right and what is wrong for he has a conscience...it's the voice of the soul, it's the gift of the spirit, it's the treasure of all men, it's the light of Christ. When it speaks, don't interrupt.

This life isn't designed for emptiness, but is detailed for cultivation and growth. When one does less than he is capable of doing, it relates to disappointment and failure. Happiness is the channel of escape from a state of despair and self-extinction. It's a rebound from honest and productive work. Everyone becomes his own gardener. He cultivates best as he lives to help live, for in the process a new branch is added to his tree of life, bearing choice fruit, bringing fullness to the heart and joy to living.

With the many disappointments of life, there comes the necessity of making needed adjustments. And remarkable are those who adjust to the inner feelings of themselves, to their surroundings, to their families and friends, adjusting to the opportunities of growth and the gift of understanding, of the in-depth purpose of life, of being mindful and attuning themselves to the feelings and needs of others.

Within the homes of the people, leaders of nations may envision the power and the strength of their country, but it's within the hearts of the righteous that the Lord calculates the strength of His Kingdom. People can live almost anywhere if things are right within. The Lord has given treasures of lasting value, yet from his storehouse of abundance, we hold on to so little. His gifts are waiting to be gathered, and should we fail to receive them in the spirit of humility and thanksgiving, they become lost beyond recall.

The personality and characteristics of one who departs this life remain constant as he passes through the door and takes up residence in the realm of the spirit world. This geographical change does not bring a change in attitudes or opinions, no change in identity. It is recorded in scriptures: "That same spirit which doeth possess your bodies at the time ye go out of this life, that same spirit will have power to possess your body in that eternal world."

This life is the day of the people's choice. It's on-the-job training. It's man's allotted time to control his behavior and overcome the evils of the world; to enhance the spirit. Sin by its very nature is inseparably connected with the actions of men. Sin is where the flesh and the spirit unite in a venture of self-destruction. Those who pass this way seem to have that built-in desire to live longer than the desire to live well.

MAN

There comes a time to plant and a season to harvest. Leaves have their hour to fall and flowers their day to wither. Everyone will have his appointed hour with destiny...the great judgment.

Someday we will understand those things which today we inquired about, for we are not without the responsibility to that which we are fashioned to become. Everyone by choice designs his own interior decorations, building within the soul a living quarters for either a state of heaven or hell.

We are a biological product, making us a meddlesome and inquiring people. We refuse to be standardized and placed in a certain slot to be measured for size. We have the complications of a body and spirit to control and regulate. Man must be obedient to the laws of the Lord if he would relate to the person he was created to become, for the future has promise...man's final state of living will be in the resurrected state.

The scriptures tell us from whence we came and where we have been, but we alone will determine where we are going, on which side of the problems our mistakes will be made.

We are a strange combination of good and evil, and should we waste our days on earth, we betray life. If we become reckless with our health, we defile the body. If we are careless with our thoughts and deeds, we condemn the soul.

Good deeds performed will outlast the performer. Truth never descends. Man must rise to the level of truth if he would do business in its name. Man is on trial, not truth, for truth is a proud name.

Among the many creations of the Lord, man alone is the only specie that brings into existence and originates and stirs up rebellious conflicts in his demands. In bringing about contention among his fellow travelers, he is an expert in his line of work. Somerset Maugham said: ''Life is short, nature is hostile and man ridiculous.'' It seems that some are born with a built-in arrogance and self-domineering lust for power, yet it so happens that man is the very purpose for which this earth was organized and put together. He stands high on the list and is of great worth in the sight of God, for he is made up of a substance that is redeemable and everlasting.

A tree depends on the depth of its roots for growth and beauty, and we must rely on the reach of our thoughts and behavior for acceptance and usefulness. We have great potential of becoming...if we are not one with the Lord, we are not one with anybody.

Love is the searchlight by which we penetrate into the hearts of others.

NEW PATHS

The most noticeable lawn in my neighborhood is one that has a path worn through its constant use, that leads from one neighbor's home to another. This lawn is put to its best use as it speaks in silence, for its potentials in providing new crosscuts where there was no path before. This pathway is being used in building friendship and understanding between families, pointing the way to secure and enjoy the gifts of the spirit, values of worth reaching above those deceptive things of the world that "pass." Too much time is spent building walls instead of making new channels of friendship.

Life is measured in moments of helpfulness, in sharing goodness and kind feelings with one another. When one has given a part of himself, with a warmness of heart, in lifting others along the way, that life has been extended. To recall pleasant moments and memories that have been spent with family and friends is to have lived twice, while reflecting on misdeeds is to have died many times.

The measure of life is in its use, not in its passing, for where beauty and love are seen, through giving and through expressions of compassion to one's fellowmen, God is revealed.

Peoples of the world spend too much time building enclosures of indifference and aloofness in place of charting new avenues of friendship. Fences may divide man's possessions on earth, but only sin and acts of neglect and transgression separate one from the treasure and gifts of heaven.

SCHOOL SPIRIT

In the early part of this 20th century the Salt Lake School Board had erected a modern building. It was named the East High School. It was a beautiful structure; well built and maintained. From the halls of learning from this school have come many noted educators, religious leaders, musicians, athletes, community builders, city, state, and national leaders.

This school is rich in tradition. The spirit of those who have gone there has been interwoven in their children and grandchildren. The spirit and unity in friendship run high at this place of learning. It has become a landmark in Salt Lake.

A few years ago a suspected arsonist set fire to the building. Damage was near the million dollar mark. The school board met. Decisions had to be made in a hurry as to what should be done with the building. It was in the spring of the year. The question came up, would it be best to tear the remainder of the building down and rebuild, try to remodel, or move elsewhere and build a new structure?

Before the smoke had cleared away the students rallied. They didn't want a new building, they wanted to restore and keep what they had. The next day they began cleaning up the mess. They worked many hours and days without any thought of pay. The school board also caught the spirit and a decision was made to restore and rebuild the lost portion.

The building was ready for the fall term, but more important, the spirit of the community was also renewed. The students had intercepted and captured the future by taking hold of the present. They held on to that which was theirs. They worked and lived for a principle. The building survival was the power of oneness among the students.

The moving cause of their action was in their faith that it cold be done. And because of their spiritual awareness, they were awakened to the fact that something important in their lives, the lives of their parents and grandparents was about to be lost and they could save it. The best within the hearts of these young students emerged to the surface and they gave an accounting. They accepted the challenge that "This thing we must do."

Property rights become human rights tied up in property. Had this stately structure with its in-depth traditions been destroyed, it would have cut deeply and placed scars on those it had served so well.

THANKSGIVING AMERICA

The meaning of Thanksgiving is bigger than words, deeper than anticipation, and greater than the preparation of food. Thanksgiving is acknowledgment, acceptance, and living the message in the song: "Praise God From Whom All Blessings Flow." In gratitude for the blessings of life, this day becomes the "Sabbath of the Year." Those who catch the spirit of the day with each rising sun brings their own special day of giving thanks.

Thanksgiving, as we know it, was born on American soil. It was set apart in 1620 by the Puritans from Massachusetts. A great American tradition was set in motion, and we in America this 1976 Bicentennial commemorate the first Thanksgiving of the 3rd century of our independence. This day belongs to us alone, and we are indebted to pass along this deep-seated American tradition.

As the fruits of the field are gathered we should be mindful of the more abundant crop, the gathering of the gifts and fruits of life...the harvest of friends, of giving and sharing. Some gather in the gifts of the harvest early in life while others gather late. A few may drink their fill but die of spiritual thirst while the seeds of others sown in eagerness turn bad...and hungry they gather.

The question is often asked, "Where are the years of childhood, the sparkling day of youth? Where are the years of maturity...are they lost forever? What has age done to youth?" Years are not lost if the seeds of high ideals, integrity, and good character have been sown. Where are the years? We are the years. Let us give thanks for the seeds of youth and the wisdom of age.

So, in America we are blessed as we reap the harvest of years from the seeds that others have sown. Today is our point in history, our time in destiny to pass along the baton of integrity, and spiritual values that are so interwoven in the traditions of Thanksgiving. We are indebted to the Lord and responsible to the people to keep alive those freedoms bound up in our American way of life.

JESUS OF NAZARETH

Jesus of Nazareth and Alexander the Great each lived to the age of thirty-three. The events making up their day of mortality have been compared by some, but there is no similarity or parallel of purpose. The accomplishments of each stand out in contrast.

The world was too small for Alexander. At the age of thirty-three he had conquered his known world and was dead. Jesus at thirty-three was dead and resurrected, fulfilling his mission of "Life over Death." To rule the world Alexander demanded the blood of mankind. To overcome the world the Savior freely gave his blood to redeem mankind. To conquer the world the reign of Alexander was a history of forced marches; the Savior's reign was a history of "Follow Me"—an open road to Life Eternal.

The life of Alexander was an outlined plan to conquer and take away. He organized armies. The life of the Savior was one of giving, adding to. He organized kingdoms. Alexander saw the potential fighting-power of the crowd, while Jesus saw, within the heart, the needs of the individual in the crowd as a whole person, not as an individual disease. Millions suffered and died at the hands of Alexander. He was called "great." The Savior died as a God, that all men might attain greatness. The armies of Alexander were never overrun by numbers, Jesus was never overruled by intelligence. Alexander extracted his power from the people. Jesus was sustained by God his Father. Alexander built up his passing kingdom of glory on earth. Jesus, in the oneness with his Father, stands among his work and glory. The earth claims the body of Alexander for its own; the tomb of Jesus is empty. When Alexander died, word went out, "he is dead," but only once have the words been spoken, "He is Risen."

The Savior never came seeking a cause for which to die...the cause was here; it is you and I and other Alexanders.

The greatest potential for the blessing of man lies in the challenge of a re-entry into a life that will dovetail into and become a part of the divine building program of the soul.

The countdown on the calendar of time was prefigured before the foundation of this earth. The sand in the hourglass began with the Savior in mortality, counting both ways.

Alexander is one among us that is lost in the count.

THE DOLLAR SIGN

During World War II the one thing that confused and disorganized an invading army most, as the tanks rolled down unknown highways of Europe, was the changing of road signs. The enemy found themselves on detour, going the wrong way and finding themselves on "dead-end" streets and lost.

For centuries misleading road signs have dominated the highways of the human family. One of the most misleading, yet attractive, has been the dollar sign. It is the most deceptive landmark ever erected to change the course and destroy the souls of men. There is no other sign that has been so misread, yet more sought after. The dollar sign is a necessary one and is beneficial for those who understand its meaning and purpose.

The Lord set up highway "markers" centuries ago pointing the way for man to travel without getting off course. Man, however, in his greed and desire for a fast turnover and quick return, has replaced the meaning of the

Lord's Beacon Light with false information and, consequently, nations have decayed and people lost their way.

A ship can stay on course only as long as the captain keeps his compass focused on fixed stars. It's his only hope of reaching destination in both stormy and fair weather.

Just as the pre-mortal life of the spirit, before coming to this earth, is the forerunner to life here, this mortal existence is the forerunner to that important event called "death." One must die before there can be a redemption and redemption is the forerunner to the resurrection. Resurrection precedes the final judgment, which judgment will reveal man's identity and place in the Kingdom of God.

Any semaphore or sign along this circular journey called "life" that is designed to keep man from attaining the highest potentials of his becoming like unto his Father in heaven is a false sign and is a part of the Devil's work who glories in his deceptions.

Only as the divine message posted on the road signs of life becomes the travelers' "way of life" will there come a fullness of joy at the journey's end.

FINISHERS

The night George Washington marched up to the ice-filled Delaware river wasn't the ideal time to launch a boat and attempt a crossing. It was, however, the precise time to surprise the Hessians at Trenton. This surprise attack played a vital part in bringing victory and freedom to a young nation called "America."

The river became the servant and the bad weather the opportunity for Washington to strike.

On that eventful third day when the Marys headed for the tomb of the Savior, they never went to celebrate a lost cause. They had work to do. As they traveled it occurred to them that perhaps it wasn't the ideal time to fulfill their desires, for it was said by one, "Who shall roll us away the stone?" The tomb was sealed but not their faith.

Not being discouraged, they continued on, and today it is written that the greatest discovery in the history of man was made by women. "The tomb was empty." The women were told to "go quickly and tell the disciples that He is risen from the dead."

Love is self-fulfilling, it is self-discovery. The hour of this day could be our moment of eternity.

The last week of July is an unlikely time of the year to plant seeds in a western desert and expect a harvest. July is passed the season for planting. However, in 1847 the pioneers, the day after arrival in the Salt Lake Valley, counted their seeds, blessed the land, and planted with faith that the Lord would sustain their efforts. Their prayers were answered; a short crop harvested, a people survived and a western empire was born. From within their hearts came an in-depth oneness of purpose and thanksgiving to the Lord for His power and strength in sustaining them in their hour of need.

Had the Mormon pioneers waited for an ideal point in time and season of the year to leave behind all their material possessions in Nauvoo, Illinois, and head west to challenge a desert to make it "Blossom as a rose," the beautiful song, "Come, Come Ye Saints" would have been lost to the world.

When is the proper time to start a project, to build character, to improve? At what hour can we find life without interference? At what point in our lifetime can it be said: "I have settled my account with the world and now is the ideal moment to begin my long delayed intentions."

The greatest enemy of growth and fulfillment is the inclination to "put off" and delay. The element of "time" is the referee and leveler of people and events. We attain only as we find our position in life as "finishers." A neglected opportunity dies within its own lifetime. There is no recall. Opportunity comes as a springboard to living, adding new dimensions for one's capacity to do, to reach, to become, to live and appreciate.

THE GAME OF LIFE

In the competitive sport of basketball, as with the game of life, each must be played within the limits of time. When the game ends...at the final whistle, the score is locked in. From that point in time the game becomes history to be recalled only in memory.

The winners in life are people with self-determination, knowing there can be no real success unless one's good fortune is shared with others, for success is something that belongs to the people.

Great men are remembered in this life for what they have given to the world...never for what they have received, or taken away. Success is fragile and deceptive...it cannot sustain itself. It has permanence only when it is entrusted with others. In contrast there are others who outlive and are swallowed up by their success.

Man has broken the sound barrier, but it takes common sense, hard work with dedication, to penetrate the success barrier. Learning to accept defeat and disappointment is the stepping stone to the business of a successful life.

We become what we desire to become...it's an inside job.

A gentleman's agreement and success story of life is to put back more than one takes out.

IT'S GOLD!

In the year 1840, John Sutter with his Indian friends and methanics, staked out twenty-six square miles of territory in the Sacramento Valley. This was east of San Francisco where the American and Sacramento Rivers came together. It was here they built Fort Sutter. He said: "Man can fashion this place into a paradise." This place was to be Sutter's little empire.

By 1848 he had completed building a sawmill which was about fifty miles up the American River. Lumber cut from the mill was to be floated down the river to Fort Sutter. He worked the soil producing good crops of grain and fruits. He was prosperous and had big dreams for the future. His hopes, however, were soon shattered.

In the spring of 1848 one of the workmen, a Mormon by the name of Henry Bigler, found gold in the river near the sawmill. Sutter had also found gold a few weeks before, but he wasn't excited about gold. He wanted to build up his own little kingdom, he wanted happiness. He asked Bigler not to let his secret be known. Bigler agreed, but a secret being something you tell one person at a time, he told another Mormon friend who had recently been released from the U.S. Army of the Mormon Battalion.

News leaked out: "Gold! Gold! Gold from the American River." The California territory exploded. The gold rush of 1848-49 was on. People came from every radius of the earth's circumference, 42,000 by land; 39,000 by sea. Flour $400 a barrel. Sugar and coffee $4 a pound. Breakfast $43. From this American River twenty million was taken in gold. Those who took put nothing back.

There was sudden wealth, unspeakable hardships, heroes, rascals, adventurers and plodders. Those seekers for treasures brought along their own environment and

shattered the unwritten laws. Some died famous, others
infamous and unknown. They built colonies, railroads,
cities and financial empires. To many something bigger
than life had been discovered. Some moved on, address
unknown. Every day was a new beginning for some and
ending for others. They lived, admired, and perished.

When the news had leaked out that there was gold in the
American River, John Sutter had already set his roots deep,
but he couldn't withstand the avalanche of greed and lust for
riches and its power. His best plans had been frustrated and
his little empire in the Sacramento Valley, built by his own
labors, was swallowed up.

Sutter was uprooted. A tree uprooted soon dies, it's no
longer grounded. Unless man understands in depth the
purpose and meaning of life, he soon, in the stampede of
events, becomes dislodged and doesn't understand why.
History leaves examples and judgments telling us that
"growth is the only evidence of life."

The history of mankind is not a history of happiness, but
one of sorrow, heartaches and disappointments. Pages
making up happiness are mostly blank pages. He who is
alive only to the appetites and pleasures of accumulating
earthly goods becomes dead to the riches of the "Fuller
Life." Everyone needs to reserve a little energy for that
other "Select Place." It is a place beyond gold and silver
where the spiritual part of man will not rest in things
beneath itself. The higher laws of the universe will not be
questioned or distorted. Every man of integrity and purpose
will move up to a higher level of performance.

HAPPINESS

Should a person attempt to secure and demand happiness from the accumulation of money or fame, it shows up in disguise...as a stranger in deception. Potential happiness is locked within the soul, and its release comes only from the natural flow of friends, through the gifts of understanding and from the joy of helping others along the way. It can't be captured or guaranteed, or purchased on the open market. It can only be desired and sought after. It won't negotiate on conditions or favors. Happiness won't make deals. It too often travels under the guise of passing pleasures and worldly acclaim. Happiness in its true state is recognized only when operating in contrast to sin and corruption.

When society learns the values and application of sharing uplifting talents with others, only then will they catch the spirit of understanding...the purpose and reason for the endowments of life. Only then will men come into their own and recognize that it's the seemingly little things of life, in helping others adjust to the unknowns along the way that build character and relate to the joy of living. Happiness is most generally a day of activity crowded with man hours that relate to pleasure and success of others.

Happiness is deceptive and steps out of character when spotlighted by the "confusion of tongues" that is spoken so widely in this the twentieth century style.

The purpose of coming this way is to so live that the promises of the Lord are fulfilled in you. Then will happiness abound and one's "cup runneth over."

THE HEART OF MAN

The heart is a muscular organ that receives blood from the veins and sends it out through the arteries by alternate dilation and contractions. In the process of this action the heart pumps ten pints of blood every twenty-four hours through 75,000 miles of blood vessels to feed three trillion cells in the body. The heart is classified as a marvelous work and a wonder.

This muscular pump in its performance keeps the life-sustaining blood flowing to all parts of the body perpetuating the days in the life span of man. The beat of the heart, however, has its final hour and will stop.

The "heart of man" is referred to as having many expressions of thought and meaning. The "heart of something" is considered as the "center of something." A devoted and loving mothing in the home is the center and becomes the "heartbeat" of the home. The words of inspiration and understanding that are spoken from the heart relate to the spiritual part of man. How man feels within, the words he attempts to express from the way he feels within, don't always come out the same, for so much is lost in the translation. The heart is designed as a reservoir for the overflowing of and containing the beautiful and uplifting things to be used for enhancing the work and glory of God in perfecting the soul of man.

As the Lord looks into our hearts, he sees within a little world of emotions, personalities and desires; he sees the faithful, the downtrodden and those with understanding hearts. The strength and heartbeat of his kingdom is revealed.

We have often heard the expression: "After one's heart," meaning as something that pleases one perfectly. To "break one's heart" is to be overcome with grief or disappointment.

"Song of the heart" is a song of tears and romance, of love and tenderness. To have a "change of heart" is to change one's mind, affections and loyalties. To "do one's heart good" is to make one happy, to please one. To "have a heart" is to be kind and sympathetic. To "lose one's heart" is to fall in love. To "set one's heart at rest" is to set aside one's doubts, fears, or worries. "Take to heart" is to take seriously, to be troubled or grieved by. "With all one's heart" is with complete sincerity and devotion.

God the Father and his Son Jesus Christ are the great central figures of the universe. Their hearts beat as one in fulfilling their mission in bringing to pass the immortality and eternal life of man."

Hearts that are pure will blend into a oneness in the Celestial Kingdom of God.

THE HOURGLASS

Time movement or the flow of sand in the hourglass of life begins its countdown with every birth. In the life of some the sand flows more freely than in the hourglass of others. The flow or movement of time merely calculates the allotted time in which a life is lived. It's the time clock marking off and recording the life span of man, his destination in mortality. It may come as a friend to some, or to the youth of life it may come as an intruder. The hourglass is constant in recording change.

Mother nature is most consistent in bringing about change in her operations. She restyles and creates new landscapes with every season. Winter in its fury and temperament consumes and diverts the beauty of fall. The season of fall transcends the summer, and the delights of summer take over the romance of spring. With each change nothing is destroyed, it's merely a transformation in the life of nature. With each change comes a deep down newness of beauty and challenge to be enjoyed in fresh settings.

In this never-ending cycle of time one can never step into the same stream of water twice nor the same season twice, for with each movement and change in time there comes a new flow of events and matchless colors, new blends of landscapes that awakens the soul and touches the heart anew.

Everyone has his own season to live and enjoy, a time to bring a fullness to the soul, to reach out for the better life before the sand in the hourglass runs its course.

IT WAS IMPOSSIBLE

In the year 1903 Professor Langley of the Smithsonian Institute built an air machine with the aid of Government money. A group of scientists gathered to witness the flight of this new aircraft. It never left the ground. It was a failure and the scientific world came to the "final conclusion" that flight in a heavier-than-air-machine was impossible. It couldn't be done by man, and that the dream of the ages must remain unattainable.

It was in the same year after the failure of this experiment that two uneducated bicycle mechanics, by the names of Wilbur and Orville Wright, young men who had their feet on the ground and their hearts in the sky, decided to try out their contraption called the "airplane." It was December 17, 1903. The flight was successful. Reporters rushed their stories to twenty-one newspapers. Only three printed it. The story was too absurd and far-reaching, too unreal to print. The secret of air travel that eluded the ingenuity of the greatest scholars for centuries had its beginning.

The school teachers who taught Wilbur and Orvil Wright said of them: "They were bright but were unable to concentrate on their text books." These young men, with their thoughts on the mechanical blueprints and laws of the sustaining power of the air, taught themselves. It would be a mere guess to say where their skills and inspiration ended and the Lord's began. It must have been a partnership arrangement. They were too busy making history to say it couldn't be done.

The future in the travels of man was born. It would never be the same. Time and space has no limits. Man has reached the moon and a space ship speaks to earth from Mars. The world is small and neighbor countries are measured, not in distance, but in a matter of hours. A one world is on the drawing boards as man travels faster than sound. Men must learn to live together or they perish together.

The Wright brothers mastered that inner drive to succeed, and the peoples the world over are the recipients of their success. The footnotes in their life are read in every language.

By their works they refused to let death have the last word.

LOVE

Ice does not mix with water until it melts. Ice floats. Nor does water mix with steam until it gives up its properties as water and becomes steam.

Love does not mix with hate until hate gives up its properties of spite and anger and reconciles itself to things of beauty...uplifting values of content emerging into a condition called "love."

When a person talks about love or hate, it's talk about people and their behavior. Both love and hate have the know-how of extending themselves, seeking out new friends. They may tolerate one another as they work and travel together, but they never sit together at lunch time. Love in its position of strength has never tasted the poison of hate, but it has felt the heart beat of its victims...love has seen the destructive force of contempt disintegrate the soul of man.

Because love will never reverse itself or descend into its holding power to a lower position of trust, evil finds itself in a state of confusion. It stands alone and must make the first move if it would step up to the higher level of performance, be identified and become a part of the better things of life.

Truth never competes against truth nor love against love; they are competed for.

Youth may pass, beauty fade, health lost, worldly possessions slip away, and life taken; but love endures. The things relating to "time" are often over-valued because they are under-valued in relating to the riches of eternity. To waste this day destroys one's last living page in the book of life.

LEAVING YOUR MARK

A famous mountain climber in his attempt to reach the top slipped and died where he fell. His friends buried him where he lay, placing a marker over the rocky grave: "Died while climbing."

Everyone leaves a "mark" of having passed this way, a mark recorded in the "library of time." That marker on the mountainside denotes that duty required this man in that hour, to be on the climb, moving up. It's better to reach for the top even though there may come a slip, than to aim low and make it. With every step forward there comes the risk of a fall, but the greater risk is in the failure of accepting the challenge. Very few struggle for the thing they do not hope to find satisfaction in, and as we reach for that "something," we discover along the way there are other fellow climbers in readiness to reach out and cushion the fall of those who may slip.

A tree, as with the life span of the individual, is best measured when down. "A tree falls as it leans and leaves its mark where it lays," leaving a cycle of life in evidence. The measure of man is based upon that which he has measured...his willingness to leave old paths and challenge the unknown. His readiness to make new trials...a willingness to risk many falls to merely succeed but once.

The measure of man is best seen in the way he spends his idle moments...the dimensions of his service, the quality of his thought and character that is left to enhance the integrity and life of others.

VALUES

Jesus has researched heaven and earth, life and death, and carefully explored in depth the personality making up the soul of man. He knows better than anyone the weaknesses, the strength and potentials that man is capable of becoming. He controls the blueprints outlining the steps necessary for rebellious man to come back into His presence.

Saving our soul isn't easy, for we have the habit of repeating mistakes. From generation to generation we, the specie of God's greatest creation, have learned the art of recycling mistakes, repeating our greed and lust for power. The Lord continually warns his children from doing foolish things, things that if committed would destroy them in the end anyway. The Savior works for us, not against us, and should we fail to choose His way of doing things, failing to follow His instructions, it would matter little in the end what other course we may have taken.

The Lord set watch upon the head of the lowly sparrow that it wouldn't fall to the earth unnoticed, that we may measure the worth of our soul at its true value.

The most far reaching need of man is to reaffirm what the true values of life are, and to keep them entact and alive to those principles that endure. The price one pays for an article is considered its estimated value; therefore, man becomes the most valuable commodity in the universe for the price paid on the cross to redeem him from the grave. Everyone is guaranteed a resurrection and not one hair of the head shall be lost. If the Lord is concerned about the lost sheep, He is concerned about you.

WITHIN THE LIMITS OF TIME

A basketball coach gave the team his last minute instructions before going out on the playing court. He said: "Remember men, forty minutes of play and the rest of your life to think about it."

The game of basketball, as with other games, is in design to prepare those participating to compete in sportsmanship manner, to learn how to win as well as take defeat. In each particular game when the players go out on the floor, it becomes their last chance to make a first good impression before the spectators as to how well they played together under pressure as a team.

The game ends when the final whistle is blown. The score declares the winner and cheers and dissappointments are left to memory. It is then that the players may reflect on how they might have done better. "Did we follow instructions of the coach and the rules of the game?" "Did the element of time have any bearing on the outcome, or did we fail to gear our conditioning to full forty minutes of play?"

Life is a game, with people competing against people, a contest that must be played within the limits of time, no more, no less. There follows an eternity to reflect how we reacted to the rules of behavior. Each day millions of people go on hoping one great hope that they will be here tomorrow to complete their unfinished work. Man's allotted time isn't programed for him to live a fixed number of years. Life isn't on the drawing boards to be used up at a specified time, but is measured by its use. It's made up of work, play, mistakes and recoveries. The game of life, when played by the rules, can bring joy, but for those who ignore the rules it becomes late in the game. It may go into overtime...the lights go out and the life of man has been used up.

The number of days given to operate and build a life isn't always the same to all men. In the days of Noah, people lived a life span of several hundred years. A person living in that period of time could delay 100 years before starting a project, take another 100 years to do the job, and still wait another century to see how things turned out. Not with us today. There isn't that many working seasons allotted to man. There is merely time to plough the ground, dig a few potatoes, grind the wheat, crack the nuts, pick the apples and enjoy the harvest.

When the time is up, the game ends. Life is over, and like a basketball game, it's too late in the contest to change percentage points. A later generation will evaluate and measure the contributions of each player.

MIRACLE WORKERS WITHIN

The most direct and unseen force sustaining physical life is deep seeded with the functions of the body. The moment one gets overly tired, it's the workings from within that brings on sleep. Cut a vein and the blood goes to work and coagulates, a wound is healed. There is no computer equal to the built-in computer of the mind. The unseen brain adds to, rebuilds, and contains itself from the inside. The eyes are connected with the brain by 300,000 separate and private telephone lines. When beautiful landscapes are seen in the springtime, thousands of separate and distinct messages are sent to the brain, telling the size, the time of year, the color of flowers and trees, the shape, the distance, the sound of birds, and the beauties of the skies.

The sustaining elements of life originate from the unseen part within. Enjoying a peace of mind that enhances joy to living is the pulse beat of a contented heart. Reaching out to assist others brings an in depth feeling of love that generates happiness for a new "you."

The ears are fashioned with power to hear, and the eyes endowed with vision to see. Within the heart is the gift of love, and within ones self is the power to be. The mind is constructed with power to do, but the Atonement of Christ is God's greatest gift to you.

TIME OF LIFE

It has been calculated that if a Honey Bee lived sufficient years to produce a pound of honey, it would travel a distance of 50,000 miles. Yet a Bee's quota of honey, for a working period of six weeks, is a mere teaspoonful; it's then through and all finished. Its allotted time for a life of usefulness is used up and it dies.

Most business firms retire an employee at the age of sixty-five. At this point in service, from a business point of view, he is considered all through, finished. His quota of time is spent, having done his best work.

In the realm of spiritual things the time allotted for man's usefulness isn't related to a date on the calendar. Because a person has lived a fullness of years isn't reason to imply he must retire from that inner feeling to improve himself and press forward. A person having used up a specified number of days is no point in time to suppress the workings of the spirit...shifting it into a "low gear status." An understanding heart relates to the spiritual part of man...it's self contained in desires to grow within.

Failure in doing one's best isn't something new, but it must be considered and taken into account for "failure" has been so successful. Spiritual failure comes without pattern or design...it's depressing, lifeless and unsound...it's seen operating in the strangest places.

Only as one discovers the purpose of life does he understand the reason for death to move in. Today is the growing season. Who is to say when man should retire his desire, his integrity, his impulse and attachment to the better things of life?

Faith is a word that cannot be retired from the vocabulary of man. Only through the spirit of love will there come from the Lord a fullness to the joys of living...to those many things promised that the "eye has not seen nor the ear heard."

The life of man never extends beyond the age of "past feelings." He may become too old to see, but with a fullness of heart for the better things in life, he never becomes too old to shed tears...to be touched by the spirit and the goodness of others.

TIME, THE VINDICATOR OF TRUTH

Thomas Jefferson purchased from France all the land between the Mississippi River and the Rocky Mountains at the rate of four cents an acre. He paid $15,000,000 for what is called the Louisiana Purchase. It was in 1803 and Napoleon of France was anticipating a war with England and money was needed; a sale was made. Today it's the richest food producing land on earth.

This sale didn't please everyone in congress for there were twenty-five members of the House of Representatives and five members of the Senate who voted against the purchase. They charged Jefferson of wasting the people's money.

In 1867 Russia was expecting a war with England, and lacking money to finance it, they made a deal with Andrew Johnson, then President of the United States, to purchase 590,000 square miles from Russia for $12.25 per square mile. Today it is called the State of Alaska.

Andrew Johnson was considered by many people as a weak and inefficient president. According to members of congress he had squandered $7,200,000 to purchase the territory of Alaska. Members of congress were upset and started proceedings to impeach and remove him from office. Johnson was also charged with breaking the law of the land by dismissing from his cabinet the Secretary of War, Edwin M. Stanton. Congress had previously passed an unconstitutional measure known as "tenure" of office. This law read that a President couldn't dismiss a cabinet member without the approval of the Senate.

The law was judged as unconstitutional, and Johnson preserved the "right of the President" to run his executive office. He was saved by one vote in the Senate from being thrown out of office.

How ridiculous it would seem today if the President of our Country couldn't choose and dismiss cabinet members without the permission of congress.

Time is the great vindicator of truth, justice and events. It has its way of measuring values of yesterday as related with today's business. As the ink ran dry upon signing of those historic documents, time was on the side of Presidents Jefferson and Johnson. The passing years have sealed up their vision and conviction that what they did was right, and so today history speaks to us in fulfilling their day in the dimensions of time. Their contributions were made under protest, doing that which was necessary for the blessing of the people in our time. They built for the future. Their works of the past remain on "time deposit" from which daily interest is drawn. They are alive and with us today, having fulfilled that inner urge of cementing together their convictions and decisions for us to retain and build upon.

ALIVE AND RESPONSIBLE

A noted speaker once said: "There is one thing we know for sure about life, and that is, none of us will get out of it alive."

Reflecting upon the far reaching side of this statement, I believe all men are much alive as they leave this spaceship planet on the spiritual flight home; alive to responsiblities; past mistakes and present desires. Alive to the challenge of new beginnings in another setting among the families of disembodied souls.

The Savior, between crucifixion and resurrection, made a three day mission stop at the place called "Paradise;" "...He went and preached unto the spirits in prison." His Gospel was introduced and the agency of choice was set in motion.

God is no respector of persons, but he is a great respector of TIME. Every man, regardless of his date of entry into this life, will be given opportunity to accept or reject the Gospel of Jesus Christ. There is only one plan of life; all other plans are distortions. The Devil never got anyone out of trouble. Only when a departing spirit understands the Lord's way will he no longer be a stranger unto himself.

Passing through the one-way door called "death" for a continuance of life in Paradise, in no way takes away or destroys the credentials and personality of man. He is what he is when he takes leave of absence from mortality, and without makeup or pretense, he will arrive as he left. From that point forward he will progress only as he accepts and becomes valiant in the Lord's program.

The body of man is created from the dust of the earth. This framework becomes the caretaker of the spirit. The combination of the two is classified as the soul; the temple of the Lord. When the body returns to dust, out of which it was originally taken, and as it sleeps with its earthly brothers, the clods and the rocks, this mixture of the Lord's creation is much alive to purpose and design. The elements of the earth are operative, waiting in silence the call of destiny, for the appointed hour, to again reunite with the personage of the spirit making up the immortal soul of man.

People will depart this life very much alive. The Lord has spoken..."I am the way, the truth, and the life...and whosoever liveth and believeth in me shall never die...those who die in me shall not taste of death..." To be alive is not related to position or location; man is accountable...he is encompassed with responsibility in every phase of living...he "owes the Lord a debt"...that is payable only in service.

THE ART OF LEAVING

There is a story in the Bible about a man named Lot, his wife and two daughters. "The Angel hastened Lot, saying: 'Arise, take thy wife and thy two daughters, escape for thy life; look not behind thee lest thou be consumed.' But his wife looked back from behind him, and she became a pillar of salt."

Here was a lady who knew when to leave, but not how to leave. Her curiosity was stronger than the voice of an Angel and it became her undoing. (A pillar of salt has now become a monument of an unbelieving soul.)

Knowing how to leave is equally important as the timing and knowing when to make an entrance. Each passing day is another step in the process of leaving this earthly home. "The house that was built yesterday has begun to consume away." A new born child immediately begins the course that leads to the exit of mortality. Some leave sooner than others. Many depart in a hurry; others linger on. There are those who leave with dignity; others just fade away.

On the body of a dead man was found a diary, and in it was written: "I will work, I will sacrifice, I will endure, I will fight cheerfully and do my utmost as though the entire conflict depends upon me alone."

This man's name was Martin Treptow. He was a soldier killed in the battle of Chateau Thierry in 1918 in World War I. He had caught the vision and purpose of his responsibilities. If he must die he knew how to say farewell; he knew what part of himself he would leave to be remembered by. Non-essentials were not to invade his purpose for living. He was aware that "before a candle can give out light, it must be lighted." He knew how to depart, leaving his light to be seen by others.

Nathan Hale knew how to make an exit from mortality with dignity and conviction. He expressed loyalty for his country as he wrote the last entry in his diary: "I only regret that I have but one life to lose for my country." He didn't lose his life, he determined it...giving an account...making a fair exchange of his limited time in mortality for the unlimited supply of life in eternity. He was not only willing to live for a principle, but he gave his life for it. Death cut short his days, but in the process his life has spoken.

In 1852, John Ruskin wrote in his diary, "Today I promise God that I will live as though every doctrine contained in the holy scriptures is true." Before taking his leave of absence from mortality, Ruskin never permitted the unlasting and unfulfilling things to take him off course. He entrained for those reachable treasures of the Kingdom. His faith was full of promise, his integrity and character were his passport for the halls of eternity.

One of my good friends seemed to have mastered the art of knowing how to withdraw from this life. A person vacates this school house of experience but once, and this friend did it right the first time. He had recently retired from his business when he suddenly became ill. Surgery was necessary and he suffered much. Many weeks were spent in the hospital. During his final days, there were hours when hope came that he might recover. It was during the hopeful days that the doctor told the son of this man that he thought it would be safe to take a few days off with his family for a vacation in a neighboring state. The son and his family went, but within a few hours after leaving the father had a sinking spell. The family was sent for. The father wanted to see his boy once more. He knew this was the final farewell. He refused to die before his boy returned, and when he came, the dad who was too ill to speak, could however, give the O.K. signal with his hands, letting the family know that within his soul all was well. He died within minutes with a smile on his face. He died as he lived. He held on to the end with that something fine in himself. In his last moments he set free the riches of the spirit, containing within his heart a love and humility so necessary for measuring and weighing eternal values. Doing things the right way rather than doing them the easy way was in keeping with his life style to the final hour.

In the hearts of the righteous lie the real force of the resurrection.

As the Jews were about to nail Jesus to the cross, He could have called down ten legions of angels and stopped a crucifixion. That in itself would have been very impressive, but his foreordained calling as Savior and Redeemer of the world would have zeroed out.

As Jesus suffered on the cross, His divine completeness was evident in His refusal to exercise His power to escape a tortuous death. In His oneness with His Father He knew what the future would exact of Him. His mission was to be one of example and supreme sacrifice. What He permitted, at the hands of the mob, was His leave-taking method in atoning for the sins of man that man might live again.

Jesus was skilled in the manner in which He fulfilled mortal life. In His final hour, He prayed: "Forgive them, Father, for they know not what they do." He knew that life is not a complete existence, but rather another step in a journey that is to last forever; that death is merely the turn in the road where life joins eternity.

He was crucified and buried in a borrowed tomb, yet He came back in three days, and stayed among His disciples another forty. And with thousands watching, Jesus ascended into the heavens with majesty and glory. "Two men stood by them in white apparel"...saying: that Jesus..."shall so come in like manner as ye have seen him go into heaven."

The Savior was born into mortality as a babe, He lived as a perfect man, and died as a God. The souls of all men will be redeemed. The door to eternal progression has been unlocked that joy may abound in life everlasting.

The Life of the Savior was His message. It was His way of saying, "Come follow me."

ATTITUDE

The trials in meeting and overcoming the obstacles that life places on us are by their very nature a part of life itself. Many problems are overcome by changing attitudes toward people and events. When things change within, they change without. The unexpected encounters along the way are there for a purpose, and these character check points are not to be used as an alibi for failure to measure up to one's best. Failure isn't disaster. Failure with integrity relates to success. Lack of success comes home to those for not having tried.

Homer, the noted writer who, because of his lack of sight, never made excuses...he never let this handicap slow him down. He, in spite of this restriction, moved forward with success, writing from the heart. His words speak today.

Beethoven, in his deafness, never sold himself short. His music is universal...enjoyed everywhere. He gave us the best of himself. He never attempted to explain away any part of his works because of limitations and difficulties.

Robert Louis Stevenson, in his search for health, never stopped work and wrote himself off merely because his health was at the breaking point most of his life. His books today are read by young and old. The quality of his writings extended themselves high above his limitations.

The test of character declares itself in man's attitude toward the basic principles of life, toward people and events. Greatness of character lies with those who have the strength and faith of the "Job-like attitude." Job lost it all and suffered about every affliction a person could bear up under. Yet his feelings and attitude toward life, toward God, never wavered. He would not listen to the temptings of his wife who suggested that "he curse God and die." He wasn't bitter toward anyone merely because he was the victim of circumstances that laid him low.

Job refused to be taught by the ways of the world...he taught the world.

BECAUSE

Because of that inward drive and determination of will, Christopher Columbus "sailed on," and today we are living in a choice land called "America." Columbus was inspired to discover it, wise men were raised up to declare it, and "We the People" have been given the stewardship and citizenship to keep it free—keep it real, alive, and operating as a free nation.

At Palmyra, New York, in the year 1820, a boy not yet fifteen was confused as to which of several churches he should join. He inquired of the Lord in prayer. He received an answer. The heavens were opened and the process of the restoration of the Gospel of Jesus Christ was commenced in that year.

Out of the restoration came the Book of Mormon, a sacred record revealing the history of the American Indian. This history dates back to 600 B.C. This book has a story to tell, a story that the world needs and knows little of. This land of America was kept hidden from other nations for a wise purpose. Today we have a system of freedoms, incentives, and opportunities unequalled in any other place on earth.

Because of Alexander Graham Bell, and through his untiring efforts, the world has come closer together. Bell, while in the process of developing the telephone, was called a "stubborn fool," and told "it can't be done " However, because of his firmness of purpose, operating in this land of opportunities and incentives, today we have what is called the "Bell Telephone System." The passage of time has brought to pass Bell's measure of works in communication. He was true to himself and shared his talents and inner drive with the world. In his most difficult hours, he refused to quit, knowing that when growth stops, decay begins.

People struggle for that which they hope to find satisfaction in doing. It becomes a springboard to a life of new fulfillments; a code word for happiness.

BEHAVIOR OF MAN

When God created heaven and earth and placed man here, He was well pleased with His work. He designed for man a long-range program for the maximum growth of the soul, encompassing an outlined plan of life and salvation. It wasn't a plan of forced marches but one of making choices. Man could choose between good and evil, right and wrong, light and darkness, love and hate. Freedom of choice is the first great principle of intelligent life. It relates to a workable way of life in which man may come back into the presence of the Lord.

The problems of earth life from the very beginning has been centered in the behavior of man. His story of management and stewardship is full of misplaced values, tainted with passing pleasures and blunders, bringing distress and pollution to the body and mind. Schemes have been promoted that only man and the Devil could think up. In his lust for power, man has indicted himself and short-circuited his potentials for a progressive and better life.

Before the children of men can be reinstated with the Lord, there must first come a change, a pre-conditioning, a revision, an editing process of the soul. The Lord isn't interested with accumulation of goods or length of days, but He is concerned about growth, progress and destination. He wants the whole person, not a fragment. The Devil rejoices with the broken pieces.

The Lord will judge each of us according to our works, and perhaps, according to our mistakes, we will judge ourselves.

Failure in life is failure in happiness; life is the pursuit of happiness.

BROKEN PIECES

In the window of a repair shop was a sign that read: "No piece of crockery is broken beyond repair." The owner was certain, beyond question, that he had acquired the art and skill of mending together, like new, any broken piece of crockery.

Gathering up the broken pieces of a misspent life and putting them together again is the most uplifting and rewarding performance undertaken in the life of man. It reaches beyond the sunset of this day.

To refashion, reshape, and recondition a life to the Lord's way of doing things, there must be friends with concern, encouragement and with lofty ideals to give a helping hand. In bringing about a change and renewal, the Lord in His goodness must be sought in prayer. With a transformation the heart becomes full beyond words of expression. A shattered life can only be put together again in the spirit of forgiveness, humility, and in the determination of walking in the dignity of man.

The ground upon which one stands is the place to start...today is the time and now is the hour to pick up the broken pieces and start the rebuilding process. One need not look for a "Launching platform"...the platform is on standby, waiting. You are the platform.

Wasting time and talents brings its own punishment...the price comes high, for lost time isolates and stops one from becoming and measuring up to his capabilities. Only as a person becomes true to himself will he reach out and use the potentials for his becoming.

There is a perfect flower in every tiny unopened bud. The plant in its budding condition, awaits with anticipation the sunshine to unlock its beauty, bringing a loveliness to the world in perfection. Also, within the heart of every person awaits that "someone" to touch the dial, unlocking a desire within to reach that higher standard of excellence.

We never attract that which we want...we only attract that which we are.

THE BY-PRODUCT OF TIME

There has been much said about by-products. A by-product is something apart from the main article manufactured, yet it has actual value of its own.

Some years ago, while working for a sugar manufacturing company, the main article produced was sugar. Beet pulp and syrup were the secondary products. It was during the depression days when the big problem facing the company was to stay financially alive and out of the loss column. The strength of the firm depended on how well it managed the sale of the by-products. The disposition of these items determined profit or loss, success or failure. These seemingly less important products made the difference. The company operated at a profit.

So it is with life. The individual isn't always a manufacturer of a product, but all men are dealers in time. Most people have a regular job, something to accomplish within a specified number of hours. The odd moments, the gift of hours beyond a day's work are the by-products of time.

Every minute lost or wasted is a neglected by-product. Time squandered or lost could well mean the difference between success or failure, mistakes or recovery. Those extra minutes, beyond that which is used up to meet the demands of the day, are the hours designed to add dimensions to living.

Time is man's greatest asset. Today on earth is for spending and improving. And today on earth happens to be just as important as tomorrow in heaven. Man's allotted years were given to be used wisely. A day unused marks off twenty-four hours of lost opportunity.

Yesterday ended last night, but now is the accepted hour. It's the last of its kind, it won't come again bearing its gifts of opportunities. Only in the execution of today does a new world unfold with fresh beginnings.

The Lord operates on a celestial time schedule. Man performs on the stage of passing moments. There is a difference. The time zone where I live is known as "mountain standard." The Lord's time zone is celestial. It has permanence. Man loses touch with life unless his allotted time is used for growth and expansion of the soul. What he does in using up his odd moments will confirm how tall and stately he walks among men.

Within those extra hours, time is available for man to live the answer to the big question that will surely be asked: "Did you feed the hungry, clothe the naked and visit the sick?"

This earth was organized and given for the growth process of man, where the family may prepare itself for the family hour in our Father's kingdom.

We owe no one as much as we owe ourselves...we are responsible to ourselves for a place in the Celestial Glory.

COLUMBUS

The entire cost for Spain to discover America was about $6000, and upon its discovery Columbus was charged with "stupidity." "This man was stupid enough to discover a poor country instead of a rich country."

Columbus had an agreement with King Ferdinand and Queen Elizabeth of Spain that by right of discovery, he could "retain all the glory." His glory was retained even though he died in chains and poverty. For his discovery, for his courage and foresight, having been led by the spirit of the Holy Ghost, nations of the earth have honored his name.

Through his resourcefulness, perceptions and determinations, Columbus not only gave us America, but a new branch was added to his tree of life; standing tall in the forest of men.

This nation with its incentives and freedom of choice has given us the talents and contributions of the Washingtons, the Lincolns, the Edisons, the Howes, the Wright brothers, religious leaders, merchants, bankers and a multitude of other steadfast men and women; people who never cut their ties with the reality for life, liberty and pursuit of happiness. They stood firm, becoming stronger than anything life could throw at them; giving a part of themselves to those who follow.

Among men of leadership, when decisions are made, action begins and things happen, during which they never permit themselves to become prisoners of their own yesterdays, nor robbing themselves of the truth about themselves; acknowledging the Lord for what He has brought to pass, and announced Himself to be for His works of beauty and inspiration on the big canvass and landscape of His creations.

This is a day when we travel with more unrestricted speed, than those who have gone before, but as yet we have found no better place to go. They looked to the future while cultivating the little plot of ground of their choosing for a place among the elect. As with them, so it is with us, for we continually need the Great Architect of the universe to keep us on course. The Lord also needs us, the bricklayers, and our going power to do that which has to be done; that failure will not do.

BENEATH THE SURFACE

The richest gold mine in the State of Nevada was owned by a prospector who sold it for $42.00 that he might move on to the next mining camp in search of more gold. This rich ore was at rest just a few feet beneath the ground where it had patiently waited for centuries to be discovered and made useful.

Everyone has hidden treasures within, waiting to be discovered; talents that lie near the surface that need awakening. Man has been endowed with gifts to be used and shared for a multiple purpose, the purpose of refining the soul for acceptance into the Kingdom of God. The character and integrity of man is the worth of his fortune. To share love and fellowship, through the resourcefulness and capabilities of the spirit, is to warm the heart and mellow the soul. The soul is a delicate instrument. It isn't designed to rest in things beneath itself, but fashioned for growth and fulfillment.

In this complex society we deal and bargain for material gain. When compared to spiritual matters, little would be lost if we lost it all. In the process of meeting and solving the problems required of us, if we fail to awaken and put to good use those capabilities of our inner-self, we fail to enhance the purpose of coming this way.

A spiritual awakening to a sagging spirit is a gift of life.

A missing coin, an unused talent, or a lost child all lack the power and sense of direction for finding themselves. They are dependent upon others to seek them out and assist them to a restoration of their potentials. An unused talent is so near yet so far away. It is a locked-in gift reminding us that the treasures of the greatest worth are as near as the open heart and as far away as the closed mind. The talents the Lord has given us must be shared in humility to be possessed.

Through the channels of creation, each is the spiritual offspring of our Father in Heaven. We should, therefore, be alive to our identity, knowing who we are, in whose image we are a copy of, and in whose likeness we may become. Spiritual things of the universe converge on man and seek to find focus in him.

The Lord has blessed everyone with a multitude of gifts, and when developed and put to proper use, we rightfully have claim to be a part of Him. So, whatever is lost among the years, let it not be in the failure of promoting our hidden treasures; for in His goodness, He has given us an abundance of in depth values, values and gifts that when exercised and shared with others along the way, will be the means of warming the earth—bringing happiness to the hearts of men.

CYCLE

Moses was a prophet and a Hebrew. Mohammed was an Arabian. Buddha was an Indian. Socrates was a Greek, and Confucius was a Chinese. George Washington was an American. Lucifer is the Devil. Jesus is the Christ. God is the Father and we are His spiritual offspring. We are a part of something, never the whole of anything, while God the Father and His Son Jesus are the whole of all things...the great central figures in the Plan of Life and Salvation.

The cycle of mortal life was finalized and complete when Jesus came this way through birth in the flesh...living a life of perfection among men, accepting a crucifixion in death, and ascension into heaven with glory.

Jesus was nailed to the cross, but having power of life over death, he was not held to the cross. In His life He forgave those who erected the cross.

God not only created man from the dust of the earth, but He created the dust. So in reflection, the ground upon which we now stand is the most valuable piece of real estate on earth. It's from this point in time that a first step can be taken in following the pathway of the Savior in becoming a better person and by following the designed plan to receive a celestial glory in the kingdom of His presence.

Man's place and effectiveness in the kingdom will not exceed or surpass his preparation for that kingdom.

DEDUCTIONS

Having lived and grown up in a small town with a population of about 3000, I became acquainted with many people during my school activities and growing up years. In reflecting back, I recall how easy it was to get the wrong impression of certain people. As new families with boys near my age moved into the community, and before I had become acquainted with them I formed certain opinions; some good and others questionable. One person in particular I thought was conceited, self-centered and peacockish. When I was introduced to him and we became good friends, the first opinions I had of him were forced to move over in my mind making room for the more uplifting feelings about him. He was a different person, not because there had come a change in him, but because of him there came a change in me.

It was later in life when this friend and I were hired by the same business firm. For several years we worked together in the same office. It was during this period that I began to see the more lofty traits of his character and began to feel of his inner spirit and the concern he had for others...his challenging ideas and purpose for his coming this way. Through this close association, I caught the spirit of his wholesome outlook. In reflection I walked in his "same moccasins" so to speak. Again there came into focus a more far reaching regard for this friend...in his growth to a higher level of performance as an example for others.

It's difficult to fully know and understand a person as he really is. Over the "long haul" of living the element of time has its own method of bringing change to the hearts of men. The decisions made at the "crossroads" of life relate to either growth or a deceleration of the spirit. Each decision brings change to the personality of man from which some talents are set free while others are locked in.

As life moves on we must accept our friends for what they are and be tolerant with those who fail to measure up to our standards and judgments. We may be low on their scale of assessment and yardstick of classification.

The photographer takes a picture of man as he appears in the lense of the camera. The artist with his brush brings out the character lines in man as he would like him to appear. At the Judgment seat man will reveal himself as he is.

It was Esau who sold his birthright to Jacob for a mess of pottage...when there was enough for both. He lost his sense of direction, destroying something fine in himself...selling his "right to become" and is remembered today among men for that which he might have been.

It was the Prodigal Son who squandered his inheritance, leaving nothing but the husks to feed upon. In his "living it up" he lost his earthly treasures, his way of life. In the process of returning home he found himself with an appreciation, realizing that his greatest gifts were within his reach...his family, friends and associates.

Judas, who betrayed the Savior, had his moments. He sold himself for thirty pieces of silver, and in the transaction lost it all...losing his soul. He isolated himself from the only power that could save him...closing the door to Life Eternal.

MUSIC

In Biblical times there was a day when all men spoke and understood the same language...then came the "confusion of tongues" at the Tower of Babel. Disorder and commotion followed.

In this the 20th Century with many languages that are spoken, there is one hope that people seek...to live in a day when all men will hear and understand the same message.

There is a language, however, that transcends all others. It's universal...it's the voice of music, the language of song. Inspiring music rises above and by-passes the "confusion of tongues" with melodies that are understood and spoken in song, in every language...touching the hearts of people the world over.

In its beginning the sound of music was introduced in the form of rhythm. It was the first expression of man, echoing the constant throbbing of the heartbeat in regular pulse. Melody soon followed to express joy, sorrow, anger and love. An involuntary outcry of the voice emerged and the voice was later translated into voluntary vocalizing, expressing the feelings of the heart. Following this, it was only natural to imitate these sounds and range of voice by other means. One by one musical instruments appeared. Then came chord structure, as we know it today, making up rhythm, melody and harmony.

Just as there are basic laws that music must follow to keep it from becoming discord, there are also divine laws that man must follow to illuminate the beauties of the Lord's creations in promoting life and growth.

Music is essentially vibration, making up wave lengths to produce certain tones...and the Lord is the lengthened shadow of man, and He has set the guide lines for a life of beauty, melody and happiness.

Strike a piece of metal to the degree it will vibrate 440 times a second and you will hear what is called "A-440 pitch" in sound. A-440 is a fundamental law relating to sound and vibration...it's the pitch and standard from which music operates under predictable and established laws.

Strike up the chord of harmony and vibrations with the Lord, and it becomes the focal point from which beautiful things begin to happen. There comes a constant heartbeat of spirit speaking to spirit, of love fulfilling the laws of love. Truth comes into focus, the voice and the soul speak, the notes of the scale come together, and the song of the heart vibrates into the heavens.

NAME KEY

Most people carry keys in their belongings. A key is merely a piece of metal that has been designed to fit a certain lock. It may open a safe, start a car, or unlock a door.

Occasionally a key gets lost, but there is one, however, that is never lost, and that's your "name key." A name is the key to one's identity and it carries the potential of unlocking many doors, both right and wrong.

There can never be another "you." There are no duplicates. And if the name representing you becomes bent out of shape or lost to the ways of the world, it can never be replaced, only repaired. One is identified by his name, which is the master key unlocking opportunities for growth of the soul. Therefore, one must be selective and particular in his performance, for that which he becomes may be tainted with that which he is.

The actions of men are recorded in a name file, and when a person's name is called, out comes the file and with it a detailed history of his performance. Written there will be stories of success and failure, good and bad, stories of mistakes and renewals. Also spotlighted will be one's love and attitudes towards others. And should the question be asked: "What did you do with your name?" the file will reveal in detail from which a judgment will come.

The great artists, Michelangelo and De Vinci, would never permit anything but their best work appear above their signature. When presenting their paintings before the public, these men would never attempt to explain away any imperfect character with the excuse they were distracted by economic conditions or other problems of the day. In their pursuit of excellence they wouldn't hesitate to destroy a year's work rather than have one imperfect character appear above their name.

Man was founded in pre-mortal existence with a spirit, added upon in this life with a body, and the combination of the two make up the soul of man. He should be more selective and particular with his creation than with any other possession. Man hasn't been granted the liberty nor the birthright to distort the divine image in whose likeness he has been created. That which is written above his signature of life will declare itself at the great judgment.

BOOK OF AVERAGE

People relate to people through performance; by what they accomplish; their works, both uplifting and works of suppression. Some people are identified and honored for integrity and purposeful goals, and others are labeled by evil designs.

When a life becomes spotlighted and passes in review, opinions are formed and judgments made.

There are men living among us who have reached great heights in serving their fellowmen. They are considered as above average in their line of work, some of whom are honored for a listing in the "Hall of Fame." The story of their achievements make up the pages in the book called "Who's Who."

There is a second group whose names are also listed in another volume of "Who's Who." They are on the "Wanted" list. Their fingerprints are sought after—not their autographs. They live off the people and are listed in the "Hall of Crimes."

The third group are the working class, the merchant, the housewife, the farmer, the builder, the teacher, and other dedicated men and women; trustworthy and steadfast people giving of themselves—giving an honest day's effort for their take-home pay. This segment of our society remains on speaking terms with themselves. They listen when the still small voice speaks. Their names are found in the "Who's Who" of the "World Book of Averages." They are the foundation upon which civilization stands.

When the right combination of the right people come together, expect a stabilization of purpose in the excellence of living.

Those who understand the difference between right and wrong have instant accountability.

NEW BEGINNINGS

The seasons of the year are continuously on the move, quietly giving with purpose and meaning to bless and sustain life. These recurring intervals seem to come and go unnoticed yet fulfilling in abundance. We also often see men and women about us operating with the same enthusiastic spirit, giving, dedicating, and assisting others in a quiet and unpretending manner.

In this choice land of America lived a man of destiny who was vigorous, yet reserved and enterprising in his efforts to succeed. He was a person on the move with ideas and results. Even though the years moved in, transforming youth into age, his mind was keen and life exciting. Work was his life, and life to him was a gift of time with a short duration of years to give an account for being here.

It was in 1915 that six of his scientific and experimental laboratories burned to the ground. His loss was estimated at five million dollars. He did he react? He responded by saying that this event was only a "turn in the road." To him it was merely a point in time to make another decision. It was an opportune time to make a new beginning, saying: "I'll make a fresh start tomorrow. No one is too old to make a fresh start."

On his sixty-seventh birthday he remarked: "I've no time for loafing, yet I shall begin to loaf when I am eighty." He died at eighty-four going full speed ahead. He was called "Tom" by his friends, and known to the world as "Edison", the inventor and genius, with the ability of doing the hardest things the easiest way...finding truth by "discovering several thousand ways that things won't work." He gave an accounting for the talents the Lord entrusted him with; fulfilling a cause so necessary to the world in helping others along the way.

Edison perfected a carbon filament for the electric bulb. When the switch was turned and the light was seen for the first time, it was likened to the "burning bush" of Moses, giving off light but never consumed, having an indestructible glow.

Very often we meet a person whose love seems to contain that never wavering glow of permanence; a love that is never consumed, yet containing the power of consuming. Such a love as it touches the hearts of people and fulfills, has a way of consuming the ingredients of hate and indifference from which is born new beginnings, reaching out for growth and sunshine.

Edison passed along and shared his gifts, and we have become the recipients. With the possessions of these gifts, he belongs to us.

ONE MORE ROUND

In the days when prize fighters fought as many as forty rounds, J. J. Corbet, then world champion, was asked the question: "What is the most important thing a fighter can do to become a Champ?" He said: "Condition yourself to fight one more round."

The world is full of champions who are remembered and honored because they prepared themselves to fight one more round, to run that extra mile.

Jack Dempsey set a goal to become the best fighter in the world. He trained, sacrificed, worked and dreamed. His greatest pleasure, as a youngster, was going from one town to another and challenging anyone in his weight class for a fight. It was his way of life to keep in condition...he wasn't born in defeat.

Dempsey lost a few fights, winning more. Every bout was a growth process in his chosen profession. He learned by necessity to plow around the obstacles he couldn't overcome. He knew what to do first; to condition himself better than his opponents. He reached his goal, becoming the heavyweight champion of the world.

In life we go all out reaching for the top called "success." When reached, we sometimes find that the pleasure while seeking it brought greater joy than when it was reached. It was this way in the life of Dempsey. A few months after winning the title from Jess Willard, there came a new sense of reality into his life. Something was missing. He realized there were no more incentives to train harder and become a better fighter, to move up...the top had been reached. There were no more rivers to cross or mountains to climb...he had been there before. There was no one left to challenge, he was to be challenged. The pleasure he received on the way up had reversed itself. The incentive to progress and improve himself was silenced.

Dempsey began to reflect and proofread his thoughts and evaluate the future. It occurred to him that no success is final. That when growth and incentives stop, decay begins. A stream of water must keep moving. If it stops, it stagnates and becomes a swamp.

Success is never the stopping point in any theatre of life. To stop is to descend...the descent may be gradual or sudden. To label "success" as one having arrived at a fixed point is counterfeit and deceptive. Many successful people travel with troubled souls...successful but unhappy. What is success? Anyone who fulfills that part of himself that he has the potential of becoming, who walks in the dignity of the person he is while in the struggle of becoming, is successful.

We can't change the past, but we can react to the present with enthusiasm...to fight one more round with a knowledge that in the battle of life there is no "last round" but merely a continuation of the same round.

MAN AND ANIMAL

Having been reared on the farm I have observed that the habits of man and animal are similar. The cat washes its face the same as man. The farmer must work the land and scratch for food the same as the chicken. When hungry, man must eat to live the same as the dog. He stores up winter potatoes and other foods the same as the squirrel and the bee. Man often sings and whistles with enthusiasm like the meadowlark. He enjoys social life getting together with friends as the ants. But when man stops to reflect upon life itself and the purpose of being here, he finds that he and the animal kingdom are unrelated in many categories.

Man, by his divine heritage, has been given his agency and the ability to make choices. He is created in the image of God and has been given the intelligence to think, to act and make decisions; but unlike the animals, he will be held accountable for his behavior. He becomes concerned and mindful about life and death, the destiny of his soul. In the business world man is paid for using his intelligence, while animals are sold by the pound. Their instincts are to stay alive and survive within their earthly kingdom, while man seeks a higher level of performance in the Kingdom of God.

Man has a "conscience that warns his as a friend before it punishes him as a judge," while the animal is void of conscience. Someone has said: "Man is the only creature that dare light a fire and live with it, because he alone has learned to put it out." There is no record of an animal counting to the figure of ten or the number of hours in a day, while man is aware of time and relates to its value and his relationship to its passing.

PREPARATION

There are scriptures telling us that this earth in its proper season and time will become celestialized and made ready for those who condition themselves for celestial living. It will be the permanent address and place of residence for those who dwell there.

This earthly planet has received its baptism by water and will receive a baptism by fire following the Millennium, "plus a little season." The meek, the pure in heart and those living the Lord's way of life will be a part of the kingdom.

Scriptures also tell us that: "This life is the time for men to prepare to meet God." In this preparation state of learning knowledge must give way to understanding of correct principles. If we lose out with the Lord there is nothing more to lose. Nothing will be more frustrating and fatal in the life of man if he fails to reach his potential glory because of neglect, his failure to complete the work at hand and leaving it half-finished. We can't outgrow the need for spiritual growth. The Lord said: "Follow me."

Preparation is the "key" enhancing the law of eternal progression. It's a process of learning, doing, of giving and accepting. We are the outgrowth of friends, teachers and experience. Progression has no stopping point...it's continuous.

The truly intelligent people of the earth are those who through their enlightened wisdom and understanding exercises intelligence enough to render obedience to the Laws of the Kingdom. This life carries with it many responsibilities. The day we cease to improve ourselves is the day we begin to die. The Lord has been generous. He has provided us with laws and highway signs as check points along the way so that we may see the state of our progress.

The three most significant words ever spoken are the words: "He is Risen." Jesus lived, he prepared, he gave, and we, without any effort, are recipients of this life and life after death. The established rules of the universe, the seasons, and the laws of nature are here for our blessings...our discipline. Try counting your blessings and you soon lose count. "Nature never breaks her own laws." She becomes the schoolmaster of all life. If we plant well in the springtime, there will come the blessings of the fall harvest.

Just as we prepare homes on earth for family life, our Father in Heaven has prepared places for his children to dwell in His Kingdom. To live is to prepare to die in the Lord, for with it comes the promise of life everlasting.

To live again can't be improved upon.

THANKSGIVING AT HOME

The words to the song, "Over the river and through the woods, to Grandmother's house we go..the horse knows the way to carry the sleigh..." were born in the spirit and anticipation of Thanksgiving. This November date is an eventful time in the lives of families as they meet to chatter and renew their oneness and love for one another, expressing their gratitude for the goodness of life.

Thanksgiving has different meanings in the lives of people, depending on age and circumstances. As a youngster with my brothers it was a full day of activities. Skating on the "old pond," sleigh riding on the hill, hunting rabbits, playing fun games and other activities.

Dinner to hungry boys was special. There were served pumpkin pies, cranberries, turkey, hot rolls, yams, assorted fruits and other appetizing foods. Indoor games would usually follow the meal and later in the evening with an abundance of food left over, we were free without questions or interference to finish off what was left.

As young boys our grasp as to the meaning of Thanksgiving was passive and fragile, but in the hearts of our parents this day was a point in time with deep meaning. This day on the calendar usually meant that the fall work was done, the harvest was in. They were mindful that just a few weeks before this day of giving thanks the pumpkins were in the field, the corn was on the stock, potatoes and apples were waiting the harvest. Wheat was in storage ready to be ground into flour. The chickens and turkeys were fed in abundance. Thanksgiving was their target date, their hour of destiny.

In their struggles over the years my parents knew it was the Lord in his goodness that had blessed them in abundance, bringing the transformation of the harvest from the open fields to the family table. This day was their hour of prayer, their day to acknowledge and show gratitude...to praise the Giver of all blessings.

My parents are remembered as ones who "were never too proud to be poor, and never too poor to give thanks to the Lord." Time was never wasted trying to discover that which had already been discovered. Their days were used up living the principles that had been tried and tested, the principles of truth. Their life is sealed up in the service of their eleven children...in the service of the Lord.

The Lord spoke to them through the spirit of the "still small voice"...they did not interrupt, the message came through. Their life was one of thanksgiving.

THE PERFECTION AND THE STRUGGLE

It isn't necessary that birds of the air call a council meeting to teach one another how to build nests, nor is it necessary that bees set up a school of instruction to teach the art of making honey. The rabbit isn't required to learn the process of changing its color from white in winter to gray in summer. The fish need not attend school to learn when and where to spawn. The bear doesn't need a calendar to know when to hibernate nor an alarm clock to announce the time to awaken. These traits and talents are inherent within the lives of birds and animals.

Animals have no other choice of doing their work than what appears to be the perfect way. To them there is no incentive to progress beyond perfection; but a poor man stumbles and falls, makes little mistakes and big ones. He has to be taught everything he knows and in the process does many things wrong.

At best it takes man a lifetime to perfect one little item or project, and then he isn't sure there aren't a dozen other ways of doing it better. Through instinct a bird cannot build its nest wrong, nor can a bee make honey less sweet, but man must have all types of blue prints if he is to do a first class job.

It would appear the flowers, the birds and animals have reached their celestial state of perfection without effort or thought. Man is just beginning. He is either on the ascent or decline.

If man is to compete with the meadowlark or other bird in song, he must keep up his music lessons. The birds have perfected their melodies. The birds have sung their best songs, the flowers have revealed their most fragrance and beauty. The dog has proven himself faithful, willing to die for his master, but man must look to the future for his perfection. He is created in the image of God and has before him the goal to reach. He receives his joy and happiness in direct relationship to the progress he is making toward this goal of perfection.

Man has before him the challenge of becoming, while the birds and animals have become.

THE FOCAL POINT
Beginnings and Endings

On the parking lot of a leading hospital there are signs that read: "Reserved for Doctors", "Reserved for Flowers", and "Reserved for Morticians." In reflection they spell out the cry of new beginnings; flowers for recovery and "make-up" preparations for the final sleep of mortality.

Hospitals become the focal point of new life and sad endings; a place where there are few people to pray with, but never a shortage to pray for. The reality of life, the hope of a continuation, and reflections of death are seen on the face of the guests.

The hospital is a good place to have been, but it's also the right place to make return visits; a place to feel the pulsebeat of doctors and nurses whose services are seen with unwavering dedication at the highest level of performance; a place where life is lengthened and pain is conquered.

A visit among the sick who have been caught in the web of unfortunate circumstances, not only brings to the heart a prayer of thanksgiving for the blessing of one's own position of health, but a feeling of gratitude to the Lord for the flow of his blessings through the hands of people who care—who add to, who give of themselves, and who in return receive uplifting satisfaction for having served with concern the needs of others.

Sometimes the best and most appreciated expressions of kindness, when visiting the sick, are the words spoken from the language of the heart; soul speaking to soul in silence, with pleasant smiles conveying the message of one's inner feelings of love. Such a visit presents the ideal moment to draw close to one another with the heart; too often words fail in their meaning.

The most welcome words to a patient are: "Tomorrow you may go home," and the less joyous: "I'm sorry, your loved one has answered the call home, having left today."

The physical values of this world are the lesser part of the values of the spiritual world.

We are put to the test. Life is a surgeon—it wounds. At times the knife is turned in the wound without anesthetic. It cuts near the heart. Pain attacks the flesh, but it also serves the spirit as it introduces the soul to a fresh new world of faith—with humility it brings people to their knees.

SUBSTITUTE

To satisfy hunger there is no substitute for food. To find happiness there is no replacement for friends. To receive a fullness of spiritual growth there is no substitute for the Lord.

What could the riches of the universe give us that it hasn't already given? What could the Lord do that he hasn't already done? Without spiritual nourishment and guidance there is little left for the soul of man to feed upon but himself. The most sustaining bread can't be made by leaving out the flour nor can the Kingdom be reached by leaving out the Lord.

To compensate for the gifts and blessings of life, mankind owes the Lord some service, a part of themselves. Uplifting thoughts merely point toward people and things until the heart awakens the soul into action in the performance of helping others along the way. The Lord can't be replaced for something less than He declares Himself to be, nor can His message of truth be interchanged for the ways of the world, and the soul of man spiritually live.

The yoke was not placed upon the oxen to give it exercise, but to divide the weight and carry the load. The Lord made it plain when he said: "Take my yoke upon you." His word is good and the invitation stands. We can team up with Him and live. Without the divine association with the Lord, without His atoning sacrifice, what else is there left for man to stake his salvation on?

The sky begins at the top of the ground not thirty feet above, and the Lord begins with those who have receptive hearts and open minds who are willing to accept His way of doing things.

To fully live is to help live. To know the truth is to live it, to speak it. To enhance beauty is to enjoy and become a part of it. To define excellence is having reached for and accepted it. To dignify life is to fulfill it.

Of all the many things we may give others to help them along the way, the least dependable is money. Within each are giveable riches.

DIGNITY OF MAN

Men have learned to fly in the air as a bird and swim under water as a fish, but their greatest fulfillment will be in that day when they learn to walk on earth in the dignity of man. Unknowingly, there are some who price themselves out of the kingdom...placing their souls in jeopardy.

As we make our entrance into this life by birth and make exit through the avenue of death, we find that it's during the interim that our character has been cast...our position of strength identified and the last line written in our book called "mortal life."

Today is our golden opportunity for spiritual growth, yet the hardest part of taking hold of and becoming a part of something that keeps growing is that it has to be done in the "now."

Man is the "representative product of the universe" and it happens that he is also the "glory and scandal" of the universe. His actions and deeds represent the best and the worst in man. Both heaven and hell are made up within the confines of his soul. Only as he enhances his behavior in doing good for the uplifting of others does he progress. He seeks pleasure when his greater reward relates to shaping destinies. Man trades each passing day for something...it may be something beautiful or something depressing, leaving its mark as a day having been lived.

Only as we quit growing spiritually do we grow old. Yet as we seek to improve ourselves, there is the risk of failure. The soul develops according to the thoughts that enter the mind. That which enters our thinking process comes back to us in its application of performance...added upon, for both good and evil. Our thoughts return to us in their appointed hour to bless or injure us. The progress of the world is the history of men who would not permit defeat to take over and speak the final word.

An intelligent person is an obedient person and his growth is the only evidence that he lives. He has only one thing to leave the world and that is the fruits of his labors.

Man finds himself between two great eternities, the past and the future. Three parties are involved...the living, the dead and those yet to be, those waiting entrance into mortality through the mothers of men. Things past belong to the past and events of the future will continue their unfolding, but today belongs to us. It is designed for a happy life.

FORWARD

He was born in 1846 and died in 1914. His friends called him "Crazy George." It was said that no successful man ever showed less promise of "getting ahead." He was unwilling to fit into and accept job opportunities of his day, but with enthusiasm he invented new ones. His professor labeled him as the student least likely to succeed. His name was George Westinghouse.

As Westinghouse was explaining his air brakes and the advantage over hand brakes to Commodore Vanderbilt, Vanderbilt replied: "Do you mean to tell me you expect to stop a train with wind? I have no time to waste on damn fools."

Air brakes are standard equipment today. Westinghouse did stop trains with compressed air and added safety to railroad travel. He reached the height of success at age twenty-four; he kept on the move. He remarked: "Work is my vacation." At an early age he recognized what life required of him. He stayed with a cause that was necessary in bringing out his best.

There is no limit in the amount of inspiration and power that may flow through a person. The only limit in the amount of power one receives is in the amount he uses.

Life is made up of right and wrong choices; the art of living is learning to tell them apart. America is a land of opportunity where the opportunity of expressing one's right of choice, is everyone's choice.

PREVAILING

Should we fail the Lord, we fail ourselves. Only when we enhance ourselves to the ways of the Lord do we add glory to His name. This is a part of the process in the life of making choices. Right choices carry right guarantees, and the wrong ones are guarantees of frustration and tragedy. When good and uplifting things are held on to, nothing can destroy them for they are embedded within, but when the things that are wrong and deceitful are embraced, nothing can save them.

One attains no real excellence without right living...without reaching out for uplifting and lofty ideals. To pick a fullness from the tree of life, one must go where the fruit is, for it grows less sweet in the barren soil of misplaced values. A tree in its abundance of giving absorbs the sunshine and becomes deep rooted and grows best in the rich soil of integrity and moral soundness.

Having love for others is a product of positive force that bears choice fruit. Showing kindness and living correct principles is a process of not only enduring to the end, but a determination of taking hold of and prevailing on the high level of righteousness.

It isn't how much we suffer for others, but how much we ease the suffering in others...not what we say, but how much we care. Life is a place where with dignity and honor we can seal up and enhance the role of friendship. We can accept people as they are and express our feeling as we are.

The greatest things in life are never spectacular in scope. The most powerful forces are those that are done quietly and unnoticed. The gentle falling of the spring rain is much more effective than the thunder and downbeat of the hail storm. Having peace of mind is much more uplifting and effective than the proud showing of earthly accumulations. Things of glamour are not to be confused with greatness nor is the applause of men to be confused with the deceptions of fame. Pride preceeds the fall.

Being known as a person of prominence is not a goal of having arrived, but it is merely a point of honor for take-off to a higher place of eminence.

TODAY

The most significant time in the life of man arrived this morning. It is called "today." Each sunrise unlocks another twenty-four hours of venture and challenge with opportunities bearing gifts designed for spiritual growth and understanding.

There comes a season to plant and a time to harvest, but this is the day of action that calls for a renewal of thought and resolve to reach and ascend to a higher spiritual level of performance.

Leaves have their falling moments and we have a date with destiny, but the most far reaching goal is becoming a part of and attaching ourselves to those principles that we can stake our salvation on. There is one source of strength and power that is reassuring to the soul as recorded in scriptures, it states: "I am the way, the truth and the life." In faith we place our trust in the Lord and with hope we enter into the plan of Life and Salvation.

We live in a day of false labels and deceptions that are unrelated to purpose and growth. Man's way of life guarantees nothing beyond this point in time...even our parents cannot guarantee us anything beyond the grave.

Congress lacks power and authority to sign into law bills relating to the salvation of man. the FBI has no jurisdiction in the matter of saving souls. Little hope emerges from the courts of justice.

The key to the fullness of life on earth and the hope of salvation in eternity is the application of truth; for truth is a quality product of the Lord that guarantees all others.

MEASURE OF LIFE

Life gets itself made up one way or the other...good or bad, rich or poor. It comes to people whether they are ready for it or not. Life isn't to be feared but to be understood. The most impressive thing about it is that everything is temporary. It passes, except the spiritual part of man, which is his divine birthright that contains its identity and personality forever.

Eternity cannot be separated from this life any more than an hour can be separated from its day or a week from its year. It isn't the question: "Will you accept life?" but "How will you accept it?" If we believe this earthly chapter is all there is to our story, we fail to see the light at the other end of the tunnel. Although life is a series of ambushes, we do have the facts necessary to make a pleasant journey. It's the interpretation of these facts, however, that presents the problems. So the question is often asked: "How do you measure life?" "By what rules?" "Is it measured by its length?" Can we say: "He who lives longest, lives best?"

The size of the canvas doesn't determine the value of the painting, nor the number of years, the worth of a life. All the Bible says about Methuselah was: "And all the days of Methuselah were 969 years and he died." The span of his years were the best known output. Death was generous for he outlived his writers, his family and associates.

Shall we measure the days of our living by the accumulation of things? Could it be that he who accumulates most, lives most? Rockefeller said: "The poorest man I know is the person who has nothing but money." A tree bears fruit, not for its own use, but to sustain others. Its purpose is to give of itself, and the children of men have no less responsibility.

Can it be said that the happiness of our years are measured by power and position? Napoleon who had world power for twenty-five years made the statement: "I have never known six happy days in my life."

From within is happiness born. It comes into full bloom in its sharing with others. Power and position are unrelated to that which brings peace to the mind and joy to the heart.

Can we safely say that the fullness of life is calculated by our physical well being? It isn't so. Three-fourths of the world's work is done by people who do not feel well. Helen Keller, who was born deaf, dumb and blind, after a full life of overcoming handicaps said: "I have found life so beautiful." Only as we give our best will life give us strength and the capacity to understand its beauty.

Things of the spirit do not just happen, they are brought about with colors of one's own mixing. These colors should blend in with the higher gifts and ideals of the Lord's Kingdom. They should be sustained according to the laws of Him who created us. Lofty ideals and low ideals cannot be contained within at the same time. The selection of one means the rejection of the other. To merely change things on the outside doesn't guarantee everything to be right within.

To become what we are capable of becoming is man's greatest challenge. As the river runs dry, the rocks begin to show and likewise man will receive a judgment for that which he has purposely left undone. A tree is best measured when down, and so with man in the attempt of building a life; he must carefully measure before sawing, for he saws only once."

THANKSGIVING

The first recorded event of Thanksgiving dates back to Biblical times. It is recorded: "And they went out into the fields, and gathered their vineyards, and trode the grapes, and held festival, and went into the house of their God, and did eat and drink." Judges 9:27

America today is rich in history and the tradition of giving thanks as an expression of gratitude to the Lord for the gifts of life. There is no one person who is singled out and honored for having originated Thanksgiving day...it originated without a hero becoming a part of the story, as the "man of the year." Thanksgiving emerged from the hearts of the people as an outward expression of gratitude for the preservation and blessings of life to live in a productive land called "America"...a land with freedom of worship, the right to plant and cultivate and to gather the harvest. Thanksgiving continues to be a day of appreciation for the answered prayers of those who built and established a government of the people and by the people.

We who reside in America are not here because we are more favored of the Lord, or that we are wiser, or that he loves us more. We are here because at this point in history we are needed most. America has been held in reserve, on the drawing boards of time, to be discovered in this era of time...to be settled by men of courage that this nation may become an Ensign to the world as a land where the rights of man, his agency and choice are basic to civilized life. This we can be most thankful for.

THE WORD
And Its Contribution to Thought

Dr. Funk, the dictionary publisher, selected what he considered to be the ten most expressive words:

1. The most bitter.....................ALONE
2. The most reverent..............MOTHER
3. The most tragic..................DEATH
4. The most beautiful.............LOVE
5. The most cruel...................REVENGE
6. The most peaceful.............TRANQUIL
7. The saddest........................FORGOTTEN
8. The warmest.....................FRIENDSHIP
9. The coldest.........................NO
10. The most comforting..........FAITH

May I add an "eleventh" word. It's all consuming, feeding upon others; never reaching up, being self-contained and unselective it attacks everyone—the old and young. It unnerves, deprives, depresses, destroys, dampens, and starves the spirit. It preys upon the mind, being a word of dejection, of gloom and despondency. It's a tool of the Devil...it's the word

D-I-S-C-O-U-R-A-G-E-M-E-N-T

At an early age I called at the home of this intruder, and as I knocked the door flew open and a voice rang out: "GOOD MORNING! I am 'ENTHUSIASM.' 'Discouragement' has moved on—address unknown. This is my residence. Be my guest. You're welcome. Having never lived this day before, I'm excited about life. I live with intentness of purpose. I love people. Will you sit with me tonight? There is hope and promise in my household."

With that short visit, the word called "discouragement" is no longer found in my vocabulary of life. It has no claim on me. I travel light. In my place of residence this word is without a home on earth.

IN THAT HOUSE
AT THE END OF THE ROAD

There is a temple erected unto God that stands in the top of the mountains. Within the walls of this sacred place is a room where parents and children may be sealed up as family units for "time and all eternity." A Prophet of the Lord stands at the head of this program. He has been given the keys and delegated authority to carry on this most important work.

This temple is located in a beautiful city, and near this city is a town, and at a distance of a few miles is a village, and near this place at the side of the road is a storm-worn house. At the head of the family in this house presides the father with his lovely wife, who at his side carries with dignity and honor the title of "mother." In her title role she becomes the heartbeat and the apron strings of the family. With love and tenderness within the hearts of the parents and children, the weather-worn house that has so faithfully stood at attention as a sentry, becomes a home.

During the evening hours, the favorite place for exchanging ideas and reviewing the "ups and downs" of the day is the family room—the nucleus of the home. Often it is here that the children's physical enthusiasm fairly explodes. In quieter moments questions are asked and answers are given which call for more questions. During this select hour the children are free and unrestrained in expressing and revealing their innermost feelings; unfolding joy and disappointments. Frustrations are reduced to tears, and tears are shared and wounds of misunderstanding healed. During the course of the evening heartaches are sometimes seen hidden behind a smile. When the night is sealed up with prayer there comes a oneness of purpose, a calmness and peace of composure that extends hearts into new dimensions of living.

This family at the side of the road consumes the day without diluting it. They take life by the hand, so to speak, and frolic with it. Having faith there is organized life beyond this mortal existence, their way of living competes against the best of all other ways. There is joy in knowing that if they live as the Lord would have them live, they shall never meet for the last time.

This devoted family, from that village, near that town, in that city, has been sealed up as a unit to dwell in the Lord's kingdom forever. With songs from the heart they not only hold to the ideals Jesus taught, but through their examples they reveal Him; rejoicing as they mold their behavior to the likeness and glory of Him who gave them life.

From the character lines of this weathered house as it is seen from the outside and the beautiful spirits dwelling within, an overflow of love and gratitude lives as spirit speaks to spirit. The threads binding this family together are so interwoven with the promised riches of the Control Tower of the Kingdom that neither time nor distance contains the power to cut the bonds that hold them together. Love in the home is entrenched with moments that never fade and years that never die.

There are honest and upright people the world over living in unpretensious homes at the side of the road. From their dwellings come a continuous flow of love and stability. In their acknowledgment for the goodness of the Lord, and in their obedience to His laws and with a fullness of heart, they patiently wait the next forward step in the passage to time to be of greater service in launching out and surveying the kingdoms of eternity. In their dedication they have stored up wealth for both the kingdom of earth and heaven.

From the humble homes along the way, past mistakes recede and a newness evolves. "Out of the lands that are centuries old comes a new crop of corn each year."

The Lord's program is cast for eternal duration, a part of which is found among the happy families living at the side of the road, where joy comes from the giving, without measure, the best of themselves; where it isn't well with any of them until it is well with all of them.

How well it has been said by a modern Prophet, "I picture heaven to be a continuation of the ideal home."

AVERAGE

The average of something is as near the bottom as the top. It fluctuates. What is average? The average of the girls from fifty states in the 1967 Miss America contest was: age 20, height 5 feet, weight 119 pounds, yet not one girl was average.

Students in school whose marks are average are considered as having rated somewhere among the rank and file of the class—having done pretty well, not bad, a fair job. Most people who are average in their line of work are considered to be tolerable and are accepted as a stabilizing force of society. In certain specialized fields, among this working group, there are some with high ratings of accomplishments. Albert Einstein, the scientific genius, with his high quota of intelligence was, according to his wife, below average in adapting himself to many of the practical everyday things so necessary to make life more pleasant.

In the farming community where I grew up, the average yield of sugar beets per acre was figured at fourteen tons. On our farm we produced ten tons. The more successful growers raised eighteen or more tons per acre. Because of our lack of farming "know-how" our yield lowered the average. The neighbors with the higher yield were more successful because they put back and enriched the soil to balance with the harvest taken out. The less successful farmers took away more than they returned.

In the realm of spiritual behavior, the average person is without claim on the preferred holdings in the kingdom of God. The laws of heaven upon which all "blessings are predicated" are not related to averages; they relate to a higher rule of standards. There is no scale of behavior indicating that a person who is average of sub-standard in moral conduct is accepted of the Lord. Such a life is out of context with a passing grade to the celestial order of living. The status quo of the "norm" isn't good enough; in spiritual matters, it's failure. Life Eternal is the higher water mark that challenges the intelligence of him who is considered average. The Lord is concerned with exaltation and perfection of the soul.

Shake a barrel of apples and the small ones seek their own level near the bottom; the larger ones move to the top. To reach the yardstick of excellence there must come change in size, dimensions and attitude.

Losing one sheep out of a hundred is a high success average; the loss being one percent, but to the one sheep, it's a 100%; a total loss.

The average of something merely points to the middle of a group of something at a given moment.

THE START AND THE FINISH

At track meets most spectators like to sit near the place where the running events end—they like to see how the competitors finish. At most universities the circular track on which the mile race is run is so measured that it takes four laps around the track to equal the distance of a mile. The starting point and the finish line is one and the same place, but the race is won or lost by the application of speed and endurance during the four laps. Speed without the capacity to endure isn't good enough to be the winner.

Good starters and good finishers are not always the same people.

The highlight of any track meet is anticipated in the running of the mile race. It was in 1886 that this event was won by Walter George. The record time was 4 minutes 12 and 3/4 seconds—a world record that stood for 37 years. In 1923 Paavo Nurmi ran the same distance in 4 minutes and 10 seconds. This record held for another 31 years. The question has often been asked, "Will there come a runner with the ability to break the four minute mile barrier?" It came to pass. A few years ago Roger Bannister ran it in less than the "mythical" four minute mile barrier. Within three years from the time he accomplished this outstanding feat, the record for the mile event was broken 26 times by 16 runners. Today (1977) the record is held by John Walker in the unbelievable time of 3 minutes and 49.4 seconds...set in 1975.

Today another question presents itself. "What are the limitations of man? Is there a stopping point of abilities? Where are the bounds?"

The physical part of man has its bounds and limitations, but the spiritual part of him is without bounds; there is no limitation in his progress as he seeks the will of the Lord in fulfilling the laws of celestial living.

The purpose of life while traveling this circular journey is in doing that which one does best in bringing happiness to the lives of his fellowmen. There is no greater success story written. The giver in the process of giving becomes the abundant receiver. Enduring to the end in righteousness is the key to the journey.

Doing the seemingly little things well, unlocks the door of inspiration for doing big things better.

Man is the spiritual offspring of God and if the race of life is traveled according to divine rules, the family of man will return to reside with the Lord in the celestial circle as winners.

A FIXED POINT

When a surveyor was asked the question why he didn't pick up his tools and go to work, he replied, "I'm trying to locate a fixed point before launching out into the unknown."

This engineer knew without a calculated point of beginning, the further he probed into the unknown, the greater the risk of losing his sense of direction and creating confusion of property lines.

The greatest need of man while reaching out for new frontiers is to establish a point of determination that has bearing on the goal he wishes to attain and to which he may safely return.

The Lord is the fixed point from which we may safely reach out and take on new growth dimensions while surveying the inner-workings to the spiritual claims of life. We are not only the engineers as to the direction we go, but we depend upon the compass of the Creator to keep us on course. We are the leaders, but also we are students in the wilderness of confusion marking off new trails for others to build upon.

The Lord is the way, we are the travelers. To lose our way is to be out of step with Him, and to be out of step with the Lord puts us in enemy territory, a place where our performance will never look good on parade.

When character is lost, all is lost as we stand empty handed before the Lord; however, there is hope, for there awaits the gift of new beginnings. The spiritual resources designed for the abundant life are on standby waiting to be seized and enlarged upon. Living a full life has little to do with a long life, quality days supersede wasted days. Nothing is gained by watering last year's crops. Blessings follow from that which is done in the "now."

Now is the cultivation time before gathering in the first fruits of the harvest. Eternal principles are the first fruits to be picked. They are the checkpoints from which we return to the place of beginning—calculated for a fullness of glory.

REFLECTIONS

In reflecting upon the events of life there are many things that come into focus. We eat, sleep and work. We marry and raise children; some live to honor our name and others bring sorrow to our life.

We go into business; we buy, sell, trade, vote and pay taxes. In a weak moment we may cheat someone, and someone in their unguarded moment stacks the deck against us. Because of our nature, we are a strange mixture of wheat and chaff. We build or destroy. On this last excursion of mortal life, if we live long enough, we grow old, and sooner or later we die. When life is used, the "rich give up their fortunes, the beggar loses his rags, the invalid no longer needs a physician, and the laborer rests from his toil."

We came into this world without property, and we take nothing out save it be the property of truth, our intelligence, character, our works, both good and evil. On the return trip we take with us the agency of choice; to accept or reject, to grow or decay.

To live, to grow, to rear a family, to set new paths, helping the less fortunate are the necessary ingredients for the abundant life. To halt, to be satisfied is in part to die. To be alive at all involves risk. To stop seeking ideals that enhance the soul, life need not run longer.

We have artists who add beauty to life. It has been said that "some carve it out of marble, others bring it to us in song; some paint it on a canvass, while others weave it in a rug."

The most impressive artists are the humble folks, who in their daily task of making life more pleasant for others, are those doing their best to live an ordinary life well.

This life is a dress rehearsal for the closing act to be finalized on the stage of the Great Judgment. Without the Lord, man has only himself to save himself, he travels the highway of life at his own risk.

Grains of sand build mountains, moments become a year, and trifles consume a life, but only the present is up for grabs.

UNKNOWN

Snap a camera at a setting of 100th of a second and 18,000 miles of vibration in the ether of space rushes in bringing about a chemical change that records on film all colors of the scene in detail.

The vastness of the universe stands as a constant challenge for the exploration of men to reach out into the unknown. The elements of the known never stir the mind and imagination as the unknown.

Columbus discovered a new frontier and America was born. Only as we become a Columbus to our own soul will we reach out and find the land of undiscovered treasures.

The unexplored spiritual capacity of man is the most far reaching frontier to be tapped. We may not create worlds or fashion kingdoms, but we have the know-how to upgrade character and shape destiny. We build too low when our aim is less than our capacity to do.

It's the nature of man to look for new beginnings. It was the Pilgrim fathers who set sail to hostile and unknown lands to carve out a better life. The pioneers left safe homes and farms for unknown wilderness. Science reaches into the invisible world to unlock new secrets. So everyday extends a challenge for new beginnings. It may not be in the field of discovering new worlds, but the field is open to make new spiritual discoveries. There is nothing more refreshing than having a renewed spirit to make oneself a better person, for the soul of man is no larger than the life he has lived.

The spiritual roadblock into the future is made up of error and deception...the highway to new beginnings is the application of truth.

LEARNING

Children seem to progress much faster in the learning process of life than parents. Their growth comes from lessons of mistakes and miscalculations. They thrive on the "trial and error" method and the "try it again" process. Every mistake comes as a challenge, and children with their enthusiasm soon learn both the wrong and the right way of doing the little things in their special world.

Progress stops with people when they avoid doing those uplifting things they have always wanted to try but never had the courage to begin. Man often feeds upon the negative side of a new challenge seeing the "failure" sign, while others see the more positive side that spells out "success."

There was a young lad who wanted to learn something about most things. He burned his father's barn to the ground to see what a big fire would look like. It was very impressive...young Tom Edison almost burned with it.

Edison stood alone in discovering many things that didn't work. He performed ten thousand unsuccessful tests on various chemical combinations before he perfected the storage battery. Failures became his advancement. His disappointments and mistakes were harmonized into products called "success." He was unbeaten because of his gift and power to grow with what had to be done.

The progress of man is a history of taking things apart and putting them together again. It's related to many things. It's a process of creating, inventing, getting along with people, looking for the good, uplifting, seeking and giving of oneself.

Life is a cycle of seasons designed for the growth of man. Man is here for a multiple purpose. The gift of today is all there is, but it's everything. It's called "mortality," and regardless of its handicaps and failures, it's better to be than not to be.

When man leaves this place of residence, his body is left to earth, his name to posterity, and his spirit to the Lord. Yet, life as we know it, is nothing compared to what lies ahead. The Lord said: "For I will make known unto them the secrets of my will, yea, even those things which the eye has not seen, nor the ear heard, nor yet entered into the heart of man." D&C 76: 10

There is hope and there is promise that not one soul will be lost or misplaced that is worthy of a salvation.

THOUGHTS FOR TODAY

It has been said the element of "time" does not become sacred to us until we have lived it, until it has passed over us taking with it a part of ourselves. As we look and prepare for the days ahead, "time" lacks the power to diminish the gifts of the spirit that are bound up with a love for the Lord and family.

In the process of giving and taking, and that's what life is made of, time has its method of operating in taking away the imprint of youth, replacing it with age and maturity. Time is on the move, it's on the side of things that grow, on the side of truth...things that fulfill and add, too.

Time relates to love, the Father of our spirits...the light of Christ. Love is a gift that must be cultivated and nourished to motivate good works. It isn't static, for when it is given, it multiplies, putting the multiplication tables to their best use in fulfilling the needs of the soul. When the heart is right, love comes...unlimited.

It's the pleasant things encountered along the way that become the friend of age and maturity...leaving memories to be enjoyed and built upon. The good things accumulated while passing this way are placed in our memory-bank to be recalled as the need arises in the uncharted days ahead bringing pleasant memories to lighten the load. These memories become the currency for safe passage over the bridge of distress and moments of sadness that are sure to appear.

Someone has stated: "If today we are wiser, gentler, more patient and tolerant, the years have indeed been kind to us. If today we are less arrogant, if our hearts have mellowed and we seek out the good in others, life has become our friend."

Today is the season of eternity called "life."

MUST

To awaken the talents...bringing a working balance to the life of man, sufficient happiness must be generated to bear the overload of heartaches and sorrow. The stepping stones for character-building must be laid early for intelligent life to reach its fullness of glory. Along the way there must come a supply of disappointments to intensify the joy of living and a measure of failure to humble the soul.

To spiritually evolve, the meaning of success must be clarified and understood for a place of honor among lasting values. Having sufficient material wealth to share with others, and with power of restraint to control its behavior, is a growth factor in the art of living. Having in reserve a daily supply of humility, keeping the spirit of usefulness alive and manageable, brings an in depth purpose for coming this way.

Meeting head-on with the unseen events and obstacles of the day calls for a quality of firmness necessary to repress and silence counterfeits to truth, and expose the intruders of deception coming into the life of man.

Having ample love to awaken the love in others...bringing an overflow of appreciation for the gifts of this day is a "must" to condition the soul for a prepared place in the kingdom.

The events of this day become a narration that relates to success or failure in the life of man. Success stories spotlight the meaning that gives value to living and measures one's position of strength for a continuation in the life of the hereafter.

To retain more power than love; to know more about the earth than the people living in it; to display more knowledge than understanding, operates on the fringe of total disaster.